Corn Snakes

The Comprehensive Owner's Guide

FROM THE EXPERTS AT
ADVANCED VIVARIUM SYSTEMS™

By Kathy Love and Bill Love

THE HERPETOCULTURAL LIBRARY™
Advanced Vivarium Systems™
Irvine, California

Karla Austin, *Business Operations Manager*
Nick Clemente, *Special Consultant*
Kendra Strey, *Project Editor*
Jill Dupont, *Production*
Honey Winters, *Graphic Artist*
Cover and layout design concept by Michael Vincent Capozzi

Cover photos by Don Soderberg, South Mountain Reptiles (front), and Bill Love (back). The additional photographs in this book are by (courtesies given in parentheses) **Bill Love**, pp. 5, 8 (Jessica Upton), 9 (Flavio Valdez), 10 (Codty and Bill Pierce), 12, 19, 26 (Glades Herp, Inc.), 36, 43, 44, 51, 57, 58, 62 (T-Rex Products, Inc.), 71, 75, 79, 80 (Simon Fung), 82, 91, 96–98, 100, 101, 105, 106, 108, 113, 144–146, 147 (Glades Herp, Inc.), 150, 156, 157, 163, 164 (Jim Priest), 165 (Frank Pinello), 167 (Stephen Fowler), 168 (Gourmet Rodent), 170, 171 top (S. Fowler), 178, 180 (Gourmet Rodent), 181 (Jeff Risher), 182 (F. Pinello), 184 (Mark and Kim Bell), 186 top, 186 bottom (J. Risher), 188 bottom (Jim Stelpflug), 189 (Andy Barr), 190, 192 (S. Fowler), 193, 194 (Vincent Russo), 195 top, 195 bottom (Gourmet Rodent), 196 (S. Fowler), 198, 199 bottom (Mike Shiver), 200, 201 bottom, 203 (Gourmet Rodent), 205 top, 205 bottom (Steve Roylance), 208 top (Larry Keller), 208 bottom, 209 top, 209 bottom (S. Roylance), 210 top (Paul Belmore and Tammy Titus), 210 middle (J. Stelpflug), 210 bottom (J. Priest), 211 top (J. Stelpflug), 211 middle (J. Risher), 213 middle (Rich Hume); **Don Soderberg**, pp. 13 top, 148, 151, 158, 160, 161, 162, 166, 171 bottom, 175, 185, 187, 188 top, 197, 199 top, 201 top, 202, 204, 205 bottom, 209 middle, 211 bottom, 212, 213 top and bottom; **Kasi Russell** and **KJ Lodrique, Jr.**, p. 13 bottom; **Joan Alderson**, p. 14; **Charles Pritzel**, p. 172; **Tim Rainwater**, p. 179; **Daniel Bohle**, p. 191.

Copyright ©1992, 1998, 2005 by Advanced Vivarium Systems™

LCCN: 96-183295
ISBN: 1-882770-70-6

An Imprint of BowTie Press®
A Division of BowTie, Inc.
3 Burroughs
Irvine, CA 92618
www.avsbooks.com
1-866-888-5526

We want to hear from you. What books would you like to see in the future? Please feel free to write us with any comments on our AVS books.

Printed and bound in Singapore
10 9 8 7 6 5 4 3 2

CONTENTS

Dedication 4

Acknowledgments 6

1: General Information 8

2: Acquiring a Corn Snake 19

3: Basic Caging and Housing Requirements . . .35

4: Feeding 55

5: Breeding 78

6: Diseases and Disorders 121

7: Color and Pattern Variations 144

Afterword 215

Appendix 219

References 221

Index 223

About the Authors .229

DEDICATION

H. Bernard Bechtel is best known in herpetoculture as the creator of the amelanistic corn snake, but his contributions extend far beyond that narrow accomplishment. His curiosity, professionally carried-out breeding investigations spanning nearly half a century, and his personal enthusiasm almost single-handedly launched the tremendous interest and growth that the hobby is experiencing today. For years, he freely donated living specimens, many of them extremely rare and valuable at the time, to serious researchers and hobbyists alike who wished to study and further investigate the genetics of color and pattern inheritance. This is his nature: to help others add to the pool of knowledge about a subject he feels dearly about. Ironically, Bern's contributions have taken place largely in the shadow of the draconian laws of his home state. Georgia continues to forbid commerce in captive-bred offspring of obviously nonnatural color and pattern morphs of corn snakes, even in 2004.

We were fortunate to have been frequent recipients of Bechtel's generosity with specimens and knowledge over the years, and are honored to recognize his lifetime achievements by again dedicating this revised volume to him.

Bern Bechtel in his home, showing a painting given to him at the 26th All-Florida Herpetological Conference in Gainesville, Florida. It commemorates his success of the first-ever captive hatch of amelanistic corn snakes on August 31, 1961. This book is again dedicated to him and his lifelong contributions to the understanding of corn snake biology, and to herpetoculture in general.

ACKNOWLEDGMENTS

The following individuals, a true brotherhood of corn snake enthusiasts, all answered our calls for help in researching and illustrating this book. Thank you Glenn Abramczyk, Joan Alderson, Nancy Bajek, Brian Barczyk (B.H.B. Enterprises), Andy Barr, Dick & Patti Bartlett, Aaron Bauer, Dr. H. Bernard & Bette Bechtel, Mark & Kim Bell, Bill Brant (Gourmet Rodent), Jim Bridges, Mark Brown, Fred Burton, Kevin Calvey, Ken Clark, John Cole, Stephen & Jennifer Coney, Jon Coote, Jillian Cowles, John Crickmer, John Decker, Philippe & Gigi de Vosjoli, Jeff Dominguez, Susan Donoghue VMD, Bob Ehrig, Kevin Enge, Amy Fox, Dwight Good, Mark Hazel, Adrian Hemens, Joe Hiduke, Paul Hollander, Sacha Korell, Dr. Shawn Lockhart, Pat & Jerry Loll, Rob MacInnes, Michael J. McEachern (whose predecessor books from 1991 by Advanced Vivarium Systems were borrowed upon for some data), Jim McLean, John Mills, Ryan Moss, Andrew Munro, Mark Pellicer, Dave Powell, Tim Rainwater, Randy Remington, Bill Savary, P. Smith, Don Soderberg, Adam Song, Noel "Mick" Spencer, Scott Stahl DVM, Kevin Stevens (Coast to Coast Exotics), Karen & Joe Street, Stephen Stresser, Craig Trumbower, Bob Wallen, Brent Ward, and Rich Zuchowski (Serpenco).

In addition, many other people helped us with this revised edition by contributing updated information and photos and letting us photograph their animals. Thank you Tim Barken, Paul Belmore, Adam Black (Gourmet Rodent), Daniel Bohle, Richard Hume, Connie Hurley DVM, Larry Keller, KJ Lodrique, Jr., Dianne K. Parsons, Frank Pinello, Jim Priest, Charles Pritzel, Bill Reynolds, Jeff Risher, Steve Roylance, Kasi Russell, Mike Shiver, Jim Stelpflug, and Tammy Titus. We are especially grateful to Don Soderberg (South Mountain Reptiles: www.cornsnakes.net) for going the extra mile by taking many great photos of their newest corn snake morphs and allowing us to use them to beautify this updated version.

A continuous flow of information and ideas was also sifted from countless pieces of correspondence appearing in the kingsnake.com Corn Snake Forum and in Serpenco's CornSnakes.com forum. We monitor both sites, and thank Jeff Barringer, Rich Zuchowski, and the numerous corn snake people who've chosen to answer questions and share their knowledge online.

The authors alone accept full responsibility for any errors that have crept into this book by our digesting and condensing the information they provided. Photos are by the authors unless credited otherwise.

Corn snakes may have received their common name from a tendency to inhabit the corn cribs of native Americans in search of rodents.

CHAPTER 1
GENERAL INFORMATION

W hat is the best kind of pet snake in the entire world? Ideally, the snake (1) has a calm disposition around people, i.e., it isn't prone to biting, constricting, or defecating under mild stress; (2) has an attractive appearance to humans; (3) is a convenient size to handle and enjoy as a pet; (4) has space, climate, and food requirements that are easy to provide in captivity; (5) does not pose a physical danger to people; (6)

Corn snakes have long been tolerated in North America, mainly for their predation upon rodents that plague crops.

is easy to induce to reproduce and raise offspring; and (7) is genetically variable to stimulate continued fascination and expansion of interest in herpetoculture. Corn snakes pass all these tests admirably.

Each year, more corn snakes are bred in captivity than any other species of snake on earth, resulting in offspring that supply the vast majority of specimens available in the pet trade today. Remarkably, despite their current prevalence as the world's number one pet serpent species, their popularity is having negligible impact on wild corn snake populations. This is an important factor, as myriad other organisms are declining due to the pressure of mankind's domination of the planet.

The intended audience for this book spans everyone from the novice needing the basics of feeding and housing care to the seasoned veteran of "guttataculture" who wants to know the latest on breeding, genetics, and the range and history of color and pattern variations. We, the authors, have put everything we know into making this revised edition the most comprehensive publication on the subject of keeping and breeding corn snakes available.

What are Corn Snakes?

Corns are members of the large common snake family Colubridae, which includes the kings, milks, bulls, pines, garters, waters, and racers. Scientifically known as the

Corn snakes prefer to seek shelter by day under things like old piles of logs, discarded lumber, and in tree crevices.

species *Elaphe guttata*, corns share the first part of their Latin name (genus) with such familiar relatives as the black, gray, yellow, and Texas rat snakes (all races of *E. obsoleta*) and fox snakes (*E. vulpina*).

Recent taxonomic work has left many researchers favoring the move of all North American rat snakes, including the corn snakes, into the genus *Pantherophis*. Genetically, they appear to be closer in kinship to other North American colubrid snakes such as king snakes (genus *Lampropeltis*) and pine/gopher snakes (genus *Pituophis*) than to the rat snakes of Europe and Asia that will retain the genus name *Elaphe*. Don't be surprised to find corn snakes being referred to as *Pantherophis guttatus* in future publications. We have retained the genus Elaphe for this volume out of habit and familiarity to readers, rather than disagreement with the new name.

Corn snakes are medium-sized, nonvenomous constrictors that prefer to be active around dusk and early evening in habitats ranging from fields to woodlands across the southern and east-central United States. Their vernacular name was coined from their habit of frequenting the vicinities of storage structures for corn. Such places are often the breeding sites of abundant rodents, their principal prey as adults. Indeed, corn snakes thrive in close association with man's interspersed farming regions where an abundance of vermin typically thrives along the overgrown edge zones. People who collect snakes commercially have suggested that because of this widespread modern land use practice, corns may be more common per acre, at least in some agricultural regions, than they have ever been in history.

The resemblance of the checkered ventral pattern to multicolored Indian corn has also been noted as a possible source for the corn snake's vernacular name. The name red rat snake is used quite appropriately too, although some people retain this name for only the nominate subspecies, *E. guttata guttata*. This eastern U.S. population of corn snakes ranges from south-central New Jersey's Pine Barrens in the northeasternmost edge of its natural range, west to the vicinity of Reelfoot Lake in northwestern Tennessee, and south to the Atchafalaya Basin of southern Louisiana. Corn snakes live in areas to the southeast of lines connecting these points, including many of the offshore islands.

Stowaways in exotic plants exported from southern Florida are likely the source of the corn snake's introduction and establishment on Grand Cayman Island in the Caribbean and Nassau, New Providence Island, in the Bahamas.

The number of official species and subspecies existing in the *E. guttata* complex is in a state of flux—the Emory's or Great Plains rat snake now is considered by some to be a

This corn snake is lying exactly as encountered on a dirt road. Note the wavy body kinks that may be a way of disguising the snake's outline to airborne predators.

The Great Plains or Emory's rat snake *Elaphe guttata emoryi* is generally more subdued in coloration than its eastern relatives.

distinct species, *E. emoryi*; others still believe it to be only a subspecies—*E. guttata emoryi*. It lives in the south-central United States and northeastern Mexico, including most of Texas, Oklahoma, Kansas, and parts of their surrounding states. In 1994, the subspecific name *E. guttata meahllmorum* had been proposed for populations at the southeastern end of the present *emoryi* subspecies range to further split that subspecies (or species), though it hasn't been widely accepted at this time. The same applies to the isolated, far western United States race of *guttata* occurring in eastern Utah and western Colorado that has sometimes been called by the subspecific name *E. guttata intermontana*. The western races of *E. guttata* have not generally proven to be as popular in captivity as the eastern subspecies so far, primarily because of their duller, tannish-gray earthy tones.

In 2002, corns from north-central Louisiana and adjacent Texas and Arkansas were described as Slowinski's corn snake, *E. slowinskii*. Regional collectors have long recognized differences in coloration in specimens from that area, coining them Kisatchie corns. The determining factor for the new species is primarily differences in DNA that will probably not significantly impress keepers and breeders. Animals from that area readily interbreed with other known corn snakes, so whether they are deserving of special species status or not, they will probably enter the mix of "corn soup" herpetoculturally.

Elaphe emoryi intermontanus occurs as an isolated (disjunct) population in western Colorado and eastern Utah.

The Kisatchie corn is from western Louisiana and eastern Texas pine forests. It was formally described as *Elaphe slowinskii* in 2002.

These three specimens demonstrate some of the range of color variation among the race of corns formerly known as rosy rats *Elaphe guttata rosacea* from the Florida Keys.

The name rosy rat snake (*E. guttata rosacea*) appears in older literature and refers to generally smaller and paler populations of corns on the lower Florida Keys. Reigning taxonomists designate it as merely a local race in recent literature. The snakes living there exhibit variation ranging from gray or straw-yellow backgrounds with dull orange or brownish blotches to some approaching the red on red-oranges of typical mainland corns. It's possible for an experienced field collector to make an educated guess as to the insular origin of some animals by appearance alone, although this is by no means a foolproof method.

For the purposes of this book, we consider the terms corn and corn snake to take in all the above-mentioned species and subspecies.

Size and Growth

The corns in today's market are descended from stock collected from all over their natural range. Certain populations tend to consist of smaller individuals, adults at a mere 30 inches (76 cm), such as some in the lower peninsula of Florida and the Florida Keys. Others from the lower mid-Atlantic states regularly grow to a husky 5–6 feet (1.5–1.8 m). Egg clutch size and hatchling length are also influenced by the locality and genetics of their ancestors. Corns from northeastern Florida frequently lay thirty or more smallish eggs per clutch, the hatchlings of which may be a petite 9–10 inches (23–25 cm). Contrast those with the 13-inch (33 cm) and over neonates that can come from a clutch of only eight to twelve huge eggs of a Great Plains rat snake from Oklahoma. Knowing your snakes' ancestral origins may help you plan for these characteristics when choosing breeding stock.

Rapidly growing baby corns can convert up to a third of their food weight into added body mass, and they can double their lengths easily the first year. In fact, with an above-average devotion of time and feeding effort on your part, corns may achieve the minimal breeding size of about 30 inches (76 cm) at nine to ten months of age. Most keepers, however, raise their corns to sexual maturity in about eighteen to twenty months, at which time they are typically in the 36–42-inch (91–107 cm) range. Wild corns typically mature in their second or third year of growth at 3½ feet (91–107 cm) for females and 3–5 feet (107–152 cm) for males on a normal to heightened feeding regimen. Corns may shed their skins up to eight times during their first year when food is abundant. The rate slows to two to four times per year after adulthood is reached.

Adulthood is positively a factor of size, not age, in corn snakes. The youngest successfully bred female has been reliably recorded as being 27 inches (68 cm) in total length and a mere eight months of age. In this accidental mating with a sibling brother, two of the five eggs laid hatched. It's prudent to note this was a case of extremity. It should be left to the record books, not become normal husbandry practice. Reproduction by females less than 3 feet (0.9 m) in length is a strain on young corns due to the significant weight loss and dehydration affecting their barely mature bodies. Besides a tendency to lay only a few large eggs, female corn snakes' susceptibility to egg-binding and other reproductive problems is higher than normal too.

Males grow longer and heavier than females. The biggest brutes top out at 6 feet (183 cm) and about 2 pounds (nearly 1 kg) in weight. Most corns more than 4 feet (137 cm) are in fact males, and corns more than 5 feet (1.5 m) are seldom seen in captivity. This slight tendency toward downsizing may be a consequence of the vast amount of inbreeding involved in modern propagation efforts. Pairing occasional huge males with tiny females, or vice versa, has never been an insurmountable obstacle to corns mating, in our experience, except for the slight worry about one physically crushing the other in an unusually cramped cage. When you have no other overriding considerations, use the largest mates possible to infuse genes for larger size into your ongoing breeding projects.

Growth and shedding frequency steadily slow down after maturity, although they seem to continue almost imperceptibly for the duration of life. After about five years' growth, you can assume that your corn will not get significantly longer. Overall body weight also continues to keep increasing slightly after maturity, although certain old individuals stay lean all their lives. A sudden loss of bulk in an older corn may be symptomatic of a disease taking hold and should be a signal to determine the cause.

Longevity

The documented longevity record in captivity for any specimen of corn snake stands at thirty-two years and three months. Records for zoo display animals have surpassed two decades in many instances. Corns that live peaceful lives with little stress are more capable of achieving such extended life spans. This is especially true of individuals that are not part of breeding colonies whose aim is to produce mega numbers of neonates, including the physically taxing expectation of double-clutching.

Without precise figures to back these claims, the experience of all our colleagues confirms that intensive breeding causes corn snakes to age prematurely. We have personally had a few specimens in the thirteen- to fourteen-year-old range that were still successfully reproducing. Several years ago, Mark

Hazel reported that he had a sixteen-year-old female corn that is still quite prolific and going strong, laying and hatching nineteen eggs at a time. That snake has been reproducing since she was only two years old. Yet we've also seen breeding specimens at ten to twelve years of age with geriatric symptoms such as general loss of musculature, ridged backbones protruding on specimens otherwise in good weight, chronically gaping mouths, permanently cloudy eyes, and experiencing general reproductive failure for no apparent reason. We know others have undoubtedly surpassed these stated upper limits and will probably continue to do so as herpetological nutrition and husbandry techniques improve in the future.

Intelligence and Domestication

Instinct plays a large role in snakes' survival, yet *E. guttata* obviously possesses a certain ability to remember and learn too. Corn snakes excel at returning faithfully to favorite shelters and finding water sources in the wild and in captivity. They are also known to reutilize avenues of escape from cages in a fraction of the time it took them to discover them the first time. They definitely learn from negative experiences such as being nipped by the first weaned rat they tackle after a former steady diet of mice, whereby they often refuse rats of any size as prey from then on.

We've heard the frequent claims by hobbyists that their pets know and trust them by exhibiting calmer actions in their presence or while in their grasp. This issue leads into the related topic of taming and domestication. With at least six generations of captive-bred corn snakes in wide circulation today, and probably many, many more for some old traits (like the original amelanism [albinism] from the early 1960s), it's easy to conclude that whatever wild instincts the species had in nature have been bred out of them. However, we believe that while the effort of altering wild instincts toward docility toward humans is in its infancy, the small number of consecutive captive-bred generations has barely scratched the surface in this as a noticeable phenomenon. Such a primitive and useful survival mechanism as fearing or defending against larger mammals will take many more filial generations to cleanse away. Evolution can be sped up through selective breeding for calmness, but it will still probably require a greater passage of time than humans are used to considering when reaching impatiently for our current goals.

We know how anthropomorphic people tend to get at times, but we keep an open mind to the chance that there's more here than simple chemosensory recognition. We're particularly keen to hear about additional phenomena of apparent intelligence in corn snakes, especially if they include any kind of experimental method or other evidence beyond mere feelings.

CHAPTER 2

ACQUIRING A CORN SNAKE

Finding a Healthy Specimen

What do you look for in acquiring a new corn snake? That may depend on your ultimate goal. Are you simply seeking a pet or an animal that will be part of a colony you hope to induce to reproduce? But no matter what finding a healthy specimen is certainly of paramount importance to you. While it's not possible to completely guarantee a healthy, problem-free snake by examining its external appearance, look for these signs of problems or potential problems:

Alertness and Attentiveness

The snake should move deliberately, yet cautiously, flicking its tongue often to check all new environmental stimuli when held or exploring. Slow, exploratory crawling is a

This corn snake is too skinny; note its prominent backbone ridge and wrinkled skin. Avoid purchasing a specimen in this weakened condition.

normal behavior when held. It should "jump" slightly at a sudden movement nearby or a jolting vibration to the substrate or item it's perched upon.

Body Weight

A cross-section view of a healthy corn snake should resemble a plump loaf of bread, without loose folds of skin or ribs protruding, and without a backbone ridge standing out. The belly scutes should be fairly flat and squared off from the sides of the body.

Muscle Tone

The snake should feel strong and firm and be able to resist somewhat if you manipulate its body with your fingers. Check for mushy bellies and rear ends. Listless, weak specimens are always poor acquisition risks.

Stool Appearance

Stools (feces) should consist of solid brownish-black masses along with some yellowish semisolids or viscous fluids, and maybe a little clear fluid too. Strange colors such as greens or blues; blood in any form; an overly jellylike, waxy, or mushy mass; and half or more of the estimated weight of the stool represented by liquids are all signs of problems.

Defects and Scars

Avoid a snake with odd lumps, body kinks, or indentations that may indicate serious old injuries or genetic abnormalities. The best way to check for these is to run the entire length of its body through your gently closed hands to feel for irregularities. Small tail kinks alone probably won't be detrimental in a pet, but snakes with such conditions shouldn't be used for breeding. The eyes should look clear (assuming that the snake is not about to shed) and identical in size and appearance. The cloaca (vent or anus) should close tightly and be dry.

Patches of unshed skin may be indications of other problems such as too dry of a cage environment, but they are relatively harmless and correctable if they don't involve the underlying skin. The potential difficulty in treating open skin and scale infections or scrapes should be judged much as you would for comparable injuries on your own body. Old surface scars won't affect a corn's overall health or breeding, only detract from the animal's beauty.

Respiratory Infections

Listen to the snake's breathing for any hint of whistling or gurgling, and look for liquids or bubbles coming from the nostrils or mouth. A puffy or bulging throat region could also indicate a respiratory infection, which you don't want to start with in a new pet. The mouth should close snugly and have no signs of sores, scabs, or bleeding of any kind, which may be precursors of, or lead to, mouthrot (stomatitis).

External Parasites

Look for bugs attached anywhere on the snake's body. Mites are your biggest worry. They're usually red or black and tiny, like coarse pepper granules. They either cram between scales or wander slowly over the body. They harm their hosts by sucking blood, which may amount to significant volumes if a large infestation exists or if the snake is very small. They also may transmit diseases, especially if coming from a source where many other herps are housed. Look for them tucked beneath the edges of the scales bordering the eyes, in the mental groove (under the middle of the chin), or on your hands after letting the snake forcibly slide through them. Ticks are generally larger (1/16–1/4 inch long, under 2–6 mm), flat, scalelike bloodsuckers that hold on by their mouths. They're rare on corns, and their presence alone (in low numbers) is not considered an insurmountable obstacle to the prospective snake owner.

Other Factors in Choosing a Corn Snake

Besides health, other factors to consider involve a snake's past history. You may wish to find out if a specimen feeds voluntarily, and on what types of prey items, by asking the seller about its history. Snakes accustomed to accepting newborn mice, especially pre-killed thawed ones, are the handiest to obtain food for in most situations. If you're at the breeder's or seller's location, consider asking to test a baby corn by offering it food while you watch. You may not want to let it actually consume the meal if you'll be traveling with it soon, only see that it makes an attempt to eat on its own. Don't be too disappointed if it doesn't feed on command, though—it may simply be nervous or not hungry during the moment of your test.

The snake's individual temperament may also be assessed by direct handling. Keep in mind that juveniles are typically more nervous than adults. It's normal for hatchlings to defend themselves against a large, formidable object such as your approaching hand. This kind of aggression is normal and should fade quickly as they mature and learn to trust that you're not a threat to them. Adult corns virtually always have a calm demeanor, although certain rare individuals may be high-strung and nippy, especially when first held.

We have noted that when the scent of food is fresh in the air, corns may lunge for hands in mistaken excitement to grab the first moving object they see. They also have a flighty or hostile reaction if the lingering aroma of a dreaded predator, such as the last king snake (genus *Lampropeltis*) you touched, is detected on your hands. Always wash your hands before handling specimens to avoid this possible distraction.

There are advantages of acquiring a juvenile versus an adult, and vice versa. Purchasing a juvenile usually offers a choice of a greater variety in colors and patterns. You will also know the snake's approximate age and have the chance to learn some past history, like viewing the parental stock, from the vendor. These are facts that may be valuable to your future breeding plans. You'll get to see the colors blossom out on a growing juvenile and enjoy its youthful vibrancy during the first several years of life when most corns look their absolute best. Youngsters take up less space than adults, making them easier to start in plastic shoe boxes or other small cages. Relatively fewer baby corns are collected from the wild anymore, so it will probably also be captive-bred, as are most young snakes found in the pet trade nowadays. This means it's more likely to adapt to captivity easily and is less likely to be parasitized than a wild-caught snake.

Buying a hatchling has some disadvantages, though. These relatively fragile little creatures become stressed by too much attention and handling, especially by young children. This may cause them to be shy feeders or to regurgitate meals more readily within a few days of ingesting them. A low percentage of baby corns stubbornly refuse certain kinds of foods that are convenient for humans to offer, such as pinkie mice. When they are feeding and digesting meals normally, they can easily consume two to three times the number of individual items that would satisfy adults. Biweekly feedings are not a necessity but will promote rapid growth if you can afford the time and money to feed them this way. Corns mature rapidly, often in two years or less, so waiting to raise an adult shouldn't take long and is well worth the wait of starting with a baby specimen.

Older corns are big and impressive, although their colors are often duller and darker than in young adults. Healthy-looking adults may be found for sale for many reasons, but as with used cars, beware of hidden flaws such as reproductive failure. A husky 5-foot-long corn may appear to be an instant breeder size wise, but that should make you at least consider why it was not kept for breeding by the person who raised it. The one thing you can usually count on is that it doesn't have a temperament problem. Corn snakes have individual personalities, but as a rule of thumb, the species is extraordinarily mild natured at all sizes and ages. If by chance you encounter an exception to this rule, though, don't expect a very big, old animal to necessarily change radically and become tame with gentle handling and patience.

Sources for Corn Snakes

Corn snakes are either collected from the wild or bred in captivity. Wild specimens are gentle as a rule, adapt readily to captivity, and can make excellent pets. On the other hand, they may be finicky feeders and may have scars or other imperfections, less than ideal coloration, or hidden diseases and parasites. Field-collected specimens in the 18 to 30 inch (46–76 cm) size range adapt best to captivity. They are beyond the slightly delicate baby stage, yet not so old and set in their ways that adjusting to a captive environment is too stressful.

Although the plethora of captive-bred corns available today makes collecting them from nature unnecessary, there's no harm in catching and keeping wild corns. The intrinsic beauty of many normal corns is stunning. Hunting for them where they live can be fun and educational. Good places to search for corns are in disturbed habitats in the countryside and along the peripheries of agricultural fields. Rodents often thrive in such places, spawning higher numbers of the predators that eat them. Look under loose bark on large old trees, in piles of discarded logs or lumber, in hollow branches of trees, under layers of trash, and in the walls or roofs of old buildings. "Islands" of cover in otherwise open terrain such as trash or debris piles can be excellent spots to rummage through too. Slowly driving seldom-used back roads on warm, humid evenings, known as road cruising, also works well in some areas for finding corn snakes crossing or basking on the warm surface.

Corn snakes are not considered threatened in nature, except possibly in some isolated pockets of intensive human growth where virtually all wildlife has disappeared. However, they are protected in certain places, such as on very small islands that are utilized intensively by man (lower Florida Keys) or on the periphery of their range (as in the state of New Jersey). They are also protected across the entire state of Georgia because…well, no one has been able to figure that out yet.

Captive-bred specimens are easy to find. Most towns and cities have pet shops that stock herps. Mail-order breeders and dealers have ads in herp publications and on the Internet. When choosing a dealer to buy from, discuss the health aspects listed earlier by phone to determine the seller's knowledge and honesty. Ask how long he or she has been in business, and ask about references from recent satisfied customers.

When feasible, choose your animals directly from a breeder in your area at his place of business. Nothing beats selecting your corns in person where you can examine them carefully, see their parents and siblings for comparisons, and ask any pertinent questions at length. Besides ascertaining their health, you may personally double-check sexes (more on this later). Swap shows can also be good sources for corn snakes, as these events often seem to abound with a great selection of specimens at bargain prices.

If buying from hobbyist breeders at shows, especially from those who come from afar rather than dealers or breeders in business year-round, be aware that they may not be around to answer questions or help with problems after the show is over. You may acquire great animals from them, but you also may end up with hidden problems that sellers are trying to unload far from home where the problems are less likely to come back to haunt them.

When packing snakes for shipping, stuff crumpled newspaper around the cups or sacks so they can't slide or bounce around inside the shipping box. A Styrofoam-lined, heavy cardboard box (as is standard for the tropical fish industry) offers moderate temporary protection against harmful outdoor temperature fluctuations that might otherwise overheat or chill sensitive herps during transit. Chemical reaction-triggered heat packs or frozen cold packs

Transportation and Shipping

With the explosion of private hobbyists and entrepreneurs wishing to ship animals, the knowledge of how to pack shipments safely and correctly has become important to many people previously inexperienced in such matters. Any corn snake can be transported individually inside one of two types of containers that have become standards in the industry. Juveniles fit nicely inside plastic delicatessen (deli) food cups and tubs with snap-on lids and multiple air holes in the sides. Cloth sacks or sturdy pillowcases work best for specimens more than approximately 18 inches (46 cm) in length.

can be placed inside the box to help maintain a more stable temperature. Care must be taken to provide adequate ventilation because heat packs consume oxygen in the chemically reactive warming process of the dry powder in the packets.

Air freight between airports was the old reliable method of cross-country herp transport for years. Since September 11, 2001, the airlines have mostly abandoned shipping freight from unknown shippers and have made it much more difficult to become a new known shipper unless you plan to do it often on a business volume. The new hurdles make it prohibitively unattractive for private citizens who wish to send only occasional shipments. Occasional shippers may find it less troublesome to find a local reptile dealer who will ship for them for a fee.

Some large parcel services accept live harmless snakes from legitimate businesses, and sometimes private parties too, if shipments are packaged according to professional, escape-proof standards. Check with companies such as FedEx, UPS, and Airborne/DHL for policy details well in advance. Don't walk up to the counter assuming you'll be able to convince the clerk how well you packed your box of animals, and that your box should be accepted "because my friend does it like this all the time." The desk clerk is not the one who makes such decisions, and, if in doubt, will probably refuse to accept your shipment by sticking to the

Most breeders and reptile dealers use a stout cardboard outer box around a thick inner box of Styrofoam to protect animals from crushing and extreme temperatures while in transit.

company rules and thus protecting his or her job. Quite often, transport companies' rules never seem to get amended on the official policy books to allow herps, even though special waivers have been granted to numerous shippers on a case by case. Rarely does one branch of a shipping company know what another has permitted, so expect headaches if you're an occasional user of such services. Understandably, the fear all these companies have is accepting snake shipments packed in nonproven packaging methods that may allow escaped snakes to frighten employees and create chaos en route. The U.S. Postal Service still does not accept live snakes and many other herps for this same reason.

To mark a shipment properly according to federal laws, labeling on the outside of the container must adhere to the guidelines of the Lacey Act (written in 1900, amended in 1981). Although that act is supposed to govern only wildlife taken illegally from a place where it is protected and moved across a boundary (like a state line), it's widely construed as applying to all wildlife shipments within the United States regardless of origin of content. Its labeling provision states that the shipping container(s) must have (1) the name of shipper and the receiver legibly written; (2) the number of specimens and their scientific name(s); and (3) whether the animals are venomous. Labeling an interstate shipment's contents as "6 *Elaphe guttata*—nonvenomous" is complying with the Lacey Act fully. We prefer using this precise method because it makes the contents less obvious to people handling it along the way who might be afraid of snakes and thus treat the parcel improperly, or who might steal the animals.

International import and export of any live corn snakes is much more complicated and is beyond the scope of this book. Query the U.S. Fish & Wildlife Service in Washington, D.C., for more information. You can also log on to their Web site at http://www.fws.gov.

An alternative to shipping corn snakes yourself is to hire an established wildlife dealer to package and ship your animals. Expect to have to pay for such help, of course.

Acclimation

Shipping via any method is a long, bumpy ride and a somewhat traumatic experience for animals. This is especially true for baby corns, so the following advice is particularly applicable to them. Your goal is to reduce stress on your new pets in every possible way for the first few weeks or so of them settling into a new home.

Have a suitable cage ready to set up for new arrivals with the basics in place—a shelter for hiding and a container of clean water. Setting them up without cage mates is best for creating a quiet, relatively stress-free environment and for quarantine purposes. Newspaper makes a good initial cage substrate because anything shed or excreted can be found easily for examination. If the snake has some of its original cage bedding in the sack or cup it arrives in, add that under its new hide box to provide a familiar scent.

The best thing you can then do for new pets upon arrival is leave them alone for a minimum of three full days and nights! Think of it from their viewpoint—the whole universe has just been changed, and they're nervous. This is one of the hardest rules to adhere to for new corn snake owners who want to immediately examine, handle, feed, and show off a new pet. Try to resist the temptation for excessive handling. More importantly, wait until at least the fourth day to give a new corn snake a smaller-than-normal meal. Then proceed with a normal feeding routine after the first few meals have been assimilated completely without problems. Most corns would eat sooner—often right out of their shipping containers—but this is not a necessary or even a desirable plan.

Patience, patience, patience! If your baby corn came from a reputable source, it will eat voluntarily. Don't panic and worry that you'll void guarantees by waiting too long to test your new pet. The fourth day in your care is plenty soon enough to offer food for better long-term success.

Quarantine

Every new specimen is a possible source of disease and parasites that can spread through an established collection.

The best preventive medicine you can provide is to isolate a new specimen from the rest of your herps, ideally in a totally separate room for at least one shedding cycle, as a worthwhile safety precaution. During that period, which is seldom more than a couple of months, keep inspecting the new specimen for the health problems you looked for when buying the snake. Some breeders advise that six months is the minimum time to quarantine new specimens and thoroughly check them out, especially as it pertains to screening for *Cryptosporidium* (an untreatable parasite). Wash your hands thoroughly before touching any other animals, preferably in a solution of one part liquid chlorine bleach to nine parts water or with a strong germicidal soap. In addition, attend to the quarantine room after finishing the regular maintenance of the rest of your collection to minimize the likelihood of spreading a disease to healthy members of your colony.

If you have any reason to suspect a parasite problem, or even if you don't and simply wish to play it safe, this is also a good time to take a stool sample from the new snake to a veterinarian for examination. Parasites don't necessarily have to be identified down to the individual species level; the general type alone (e.g., roundworms or tapeworms) is usually enough to determine appropriate treatment. A veterinarian specializing primarily in cats and dogs should be able to perform a basic fecal exam, but not all vets will work on, or are even familiar with, herps. (You may have to search a bit to find a herp vet in your region; see ARAV in the appendix.)

If all else fails, some tests may be performed by sending samples via the mail to qualified vets located out of your area. One way or another, however, try to consult a herp vet specialist before the actual treatment commences. A vet inexperienced with reptiles might be tempted to mistakenly rely on mammalian dosages of drugs, which are usually too high for herps.

NOTE: Don't let impatience override your decision to observe a quarantine period, and especially don't fall for the old rationale, "My corn came from Gus Guttata, the world renowned breeder. I don't have to take the usual precautions knowing it came from him!" Don't let down your guard on something as simple as quarantining of all new specimens entering your collection.

Legalities

Before acquiring a corn snake, you'll need to check the laws regarding buying and keeping reptiles in your area, or even your building if you rent. Today we live with more wildlife laws than anyone can hope to know or even be fully aware of. While they are presumably well-intended, sometimes these regulations or bans are hastily conceived by people who fear or hate reptiles and can't understand that not everyone shares those feelings. Or, they think the easy solution to saving wildlife is by "protecting" it with hands-off laws. Such laws usually result in a few individuals fined or arrested annually for possessing or selling dozens of specimens, while during the same period bulldozers continue plowing tens of thousands of the same animals, and their habitats, out of existence permanently. We must try to stay aware of constantly changing regulations that may directly or indirectly affect our freedom to interact with corn snakes and other herps, even in the privacy of our own homes.

When laws concern herps, they're usually aimed at one of three different aspects: (1) protecting endangered species; (2) keeping out species that might escape and become problems should they breed and become invasive species in an area in which they do not occur naturally; and (3) avoiding having within certain communities' jurisdictions species that might frighten or injure people.

Corn snakes do not realistically fit the first description of endangered species. Despite that, they are still governed by a general wildlife protection law in Georgia that protects nearly every herp species under blanket statewide protection. It is still illegal to buy, sell, or trade corn snakes within the borders of Georgia, no matter what "nonwild" color or pattern morph they exhibit.

Category 2 was never a concern until recently, now that regulating invasive species has become the catchphrase in

Hidden Enemy

New threats to our freedom to keep corn snakes, and all other herps, loom in the form of two emergent enemies—the Humane Society of the United States (HSUS) and People for the Ethical Treatment of Animals (PETA). These closely-aligned animal rights organizations have now set their sights on the reptile hobby and trade, their ultimate goals being to stop it completely and ban the keeping of all herps as pets. In their published rhetoric, reptiles are totally unsuitable as pets. They believe that nearly all reptiles suffer and lead shortened lives when kept in cages. They go so far as to include captive-bred corn snakes in that appraisal, but not through sheer ignorance.

Their clever strategy is to focus the public's attention on isolated problems they can capture on film to evoke sympathy, and then imply that those disturbing images represent normal practices in reptile keeping. Recognizing the huge progress in herpetoculture over the past couple decades—that the majority of pet herps are already being captive-bred, not taken from the wild—would not strengthen their case to get your money. They choose to ignore captive reptile breeding so the public can be duped into believing that stopping all reptile keeping would help save all the wild animals in nature. Both of these groups now spend huge amounts of well-meaning citizens' donations to completely end the reptile hobby and trade. None of the money given to them goes to help poor animals in local Humane Society shelters; they are completely different organizations.

Washington. Don't be too surprised when, due to their hardiness and being transported globally as the most popular pet snakes of all time, they're swept into this second category by future legislation.

It's the third category that will affect the greatest number of corn snake enthusiasts today. Despite huge progress in quelling the public's fear of snakes, everyone's mind has yet to be changed. While the younger generations have embraced snakes as pets, it's the older generations that haven't all been won over. It's also mostly people in the latter age group who are writing laws.

When laws do apply, getting caught disobeying them, whether or not they seem to make any sense to you, can cause you massive and expensive headaches that are always best avoided if possible. It's wise to check with both your hometown's zoning department and the state wildlife department about any laws that affect the keeping of corn snakes in your area. Let our past experience guide you, especially with smaller local authorities, when we suggest calling anonymously, asking for the name and position of whoever speaks to you, and requesting reference numbers of any regulations they quote. This may help keep them honest when the tendency is often strong to simply say no and make the perceived nasty problem go away. Libraries usually also have sets of municipal ordinances in their reference collection where you may check on local laws that pertain to animals, and many also post the information online.

Taming Corn Snakes

Some readers may be wondering if this section is even necessary. As a species, corns tend to be calmer than most kinds of snakes—their docile temperaments are among the many reasons corn snakes are already so popular as pets. How much tamer do they need to be? That summed up our seasoned attitude when the first edition was penned. We've since come to appreciate that not everyone grew up around snakes, laughing off the inevitable nips and bites they inflict out of fear. The boom in herp keeping has brought a whole new wave of people into the hobby. They typically lack the gradual learning curve we and other contemporaries gained over many decades—things we often take for granted as intuitive regarding snakes. It is for these new hobbyists we added this topic.

Despite progress toward "domesticating" *E. guttata*, herpetoculturists can't yet boast we've achieved that goal 100 percent. That's not admitting defeat, but rather a realistic assessment of an effort that's still very much a work in progress. Corns have been bred for less than half of a century so far. Compared to millennia of refinement spent on dogs, cats, horses, chickens, goldfish, and koi, we've just begun. This is a fact that's seldom considered when opponents of reptile keeping attack with the claim that we're dealing with wild animals.

Presumed tameness is also the downfall of some enthusiasts new to the hobby. They assume that a baby albino corn snake for sale in a pet shop displayed alongside friendly parakeets and cuddly kittens must be tame. After all, pets kept by the public, by definition, must be tame. Everyone's keeping them now, so they must have been totally tamed from their wild ancestors, right?

Even the most aberrantly colored and patterned baby corn snake's natural instincts are still quite intact. It views humans as just another of many giant predators capable of making a snack of it. It's a simple survival mechanism it's been programmed with at hatching. A young corn will defend itself the only ways it knows—either fleeing or striking and shaking the tail rapidly to try and scare you away. Honed to perfection by rattlesnakes, tail vibration is also used commonly by corns (and many other snakes) to show nervousness. Failing that, they will try to bite.

The bite of a baby corn rarely punctures the skin, at most bringing a drop of blood like the prick of a sandspur. Even an adult corn can't do as much damage as a white mouse or an angry cat. But to a person under the illusion that corns advertised as pets simply don't bite, the reality is a frighteningly rude awakening. The plain truth of the matter is that some individuals have more hyper personalities than others. That applies to all animals, including other long-established pet species and even people.

Except for the initial examination you should perform when first receiving it, give your new pet corn several days to acclimate. Keep early handling sessions to only a few minutes (perhaps ten to fifteen minutes; long enough for the new pet to settle down, but no longer) at a time. Later, a quiet, extended time together while you watch TV may give it time to get used to you in a nonthreatening manner. Some people have gone as far as leaving a used clothing item such as a T-shirt in the cage of a new pet. They claim it helps the snake get used to their smell more quickly. We don't know if it works or not, but can't see that it would hurt.

When first picking up the baby, it is important to reach in confidently and slowly, but not hesitantly. Ignore any "bad behavior" such as tail rattling, striking, or biting—it is of no consequence. If you reach in and hesitate, alternately moving your hand closer and further away, you are inviting fear and anger from the scared little snake. If you really are nervous, just put on a lightweight glove temporarily and proceed as before. The first few minutes are most likely to get the most negative reaction from the corn. After that, it will probably settle down unless you do something to agitate it. Hatchlings can be pretty squirmy and fast-moving, so the first few sessions should be right over the top of the cage—a good place to fall should it wriggle away from you.

A very important suggestion is to always end each training session on a positive note. If your pet is behaving badly and you react by putting it away, you are teaching it to perform that behavior whenever it wants to return to its cage. Snakes are not extremely intelligent, but with repetition they will learn simple behaviors such as this. Is that how you would teach a child or dog to behave properly? Try to think from the snake's viewpoint whenever possible. Since we humans are supposed to be smarter than reptiles, if we have the patience we will win out with persistence.

CHAPTER 3

BASIC CAGING AND HOUSING REQUIREMENTS

Corns are masters at finding tiny spaces and squeezing into or through them. If a corn snake can escape, it will escape! Escaped snakes are a primary cause of legislation that restricts their ownership. For this reason, in addition to not wanting to lose your pet, it is your duty to do your best to prevent its escape. Using an escape-proof enclosure must be a primary consideration when purchasing or building a home for your corn snake.

The most readily available are the all-glass reptile enclosures with sliding screen tops now sold in many pet stores. The one-piece fiberglass or plastic units are also very good. Most have a sliding pin type of locking mechanism. We feel the minimum size enclosure for a single adult corn snake has the dimensions of a standard 20-gallon long aquarium—12 inches wide × 30 inches long × 12 inches high (30 cm × 76 cm × 30 cm). Even larger enclosures that will allow it to roam and exercise properly are preferable for a large adult snake.

An exception to this ideal might apply to corns between hatchling and approximately 18 inches long. For closer monitoring, they are best started in a large plastic terrarium or shoe box or a 5- to 10-gallon aquarium with sliding screened-top enclosure before graduation to a larger cage. They don't get lost in them and can be found and checked more easily for health concerns, cleaning feces, and such. If you decide to use an adult size cage for a juvenile, be sure to thoroughly check all openings and gaps, especially around sliding glass doors. They were designed to keep adult snakes in, not active little babies.

When building your own larger cage, the material used for the walls should have a smooth, nonporous surface for easy cleaning and sterilization. Glass works best, though Plexiglas, fiberglass, aluminum, or sealed wood is also satisfactory. Avoid cracks and gaps to prevent a snake from squeezing its snout into a tight space as it searches for an escape route. This can cause snout injuries, or possibly even allow the snake to partially enter the space and get stuck. Crevices along the lowest several inches are especially important to seal to prevent spilled fluids or liquid excreta from seeping in, allowing bacteria to collect and grow. Make sure that all sealants or paints are thoroughly cured so toxic fumes aren't inhaled by the cage occupant.

If the entire cage top isn't ventilated (as is a full-screen terrarium lid), make sure a minimum of two separate openings of 4 square inches (26 sq cm) each are present on different sides of the cage to provide adequate air exchange. Preferably, one opening should be lower and one higher to encourage cross-ventilation in the slightest breeze or room thermocline. The mesh covering the openings should have individual holes no larger than 1/8 inch (3 mm) and on the inside surface should present a nonabrasive texture when you rub your fingers firmly across the mesh. If the mesh

Plastic storage boxes of the 28-quart capacity are popular sizes for adult corn "cages". They can be used in custom-made tiered shelving racks that efficiently use space.

feels rough, your snake may rub its snout raw against it when exploring potential escape points.

One-piece molded plastic, glass-fronted herp cages of all sizes have become fashionable and widely available in recent years. Myriad designs offer access from front removable sliding glass or rear ceiling hatches, and with all manner of ventilation and light openings, too. Their smooth insides are easily cleaned and sterilized. Some kinds are square in profile so many similar units are stackable.

Hatchlings are most easily housed in clear or translucent plastic storage boxes with close-fitting lids. These are often marketed in department stores' housewares departments as shoe boxes. Holes of no larger than 1/8 inch (3 mm) in diameter can be melted or drilled into each of the four sides along the upper edges. The number of holes should vary according to whether you're trying to retain moisture (if you live in a dry desert climate) or trying to let the cage air out (where high relative humidity prevails, as in Florida).

Plastic boxes fit nicely into specially built shelving units in which each overhead shelf is less than 3/16 inch (4.6 mm) above the lid of the unit below it. The low overhead prevents the box lid from rising far enough to let the occupant escape. Other systems designed with closer tolerances use larger boxes without lids at all; the shelf bottom above the box acts as the lid to the cage below. The shallower kinds of units minimize unnecessary vertical space to allow more actual cages in a smaller area.

Since the units are not meant to show off specimens, it isn't important to illuminate the boxes for easy viewing. The snakes may feel more secure in the dim light with a minimum number of disturbances in such a system. These high-rise styles of economical housing were developed by private commercial colubrid snake breeders so they could maintain large numbers of specimens in their ongoing projects. Attractive professional models are now mass-produced and sold for carpentry-challenged herpetoculturists. Herp magazine ads, the Internet, and herp trade shows are excellent sources for locating manufacturers of such specialty units.

No matter what style of containment system you use, a tight-fitting door, heavily weighted-down lid, or other method of securely closing it is mandatory to prevent escapes. Corn snakes' climbing agility and expertise at squeezing out of tiny cracks and openings are nearly legendary. Small ones can even scale glass by partially adhering to it when wet. Whenever they do escape, they seem to remember how they managed it the first time. The next occurrence will usually take place in one-tenth the time it took the snake to figure it out the first time if you don't correct the situation immediately.

When corns occasionally do find their way out of their cage, their dash to freedom is often anything but fast or calculated. Try to immediately seal the room, using cloth stuffed under the door. Corn snakes, especially small ones, usually explore upward. Seek them on or inside things such as high shelves, clinging around window casings, on blinds or curtain rods, behind pictures on the wall, or in hanging plants. Search the room again with a flashlight just after dark, and then again several times during the evening and night for the best chance of finding them out exploring. Covering vents with wire mesh increases the chance of keeping the escapee in the room.

If no escape opening exists around windows or holes in walls, corns will eventually take to the floor and follow the room's perimeter until stumbling upon a doorway or crevice along the wall. You can lay toothpicks on floors near room doors to check when a wandering snake passes by and disturbs them. Powder, such as flour or salt, also works well for recording snake tracks.

Put a handful of mouse cage shavings, or actual live baby mice, in a 5-gallon bucket. Leave it on the floor next to a shelf in a room corner to attract a hungry snake to crawl down into it to consume the mice. Leave some form of shelter, such as layers of cardboard wedged in the bucket, so the snake can hide comfortably, tempting it to stay there to digest the meal.

A clever snake trap device addresses snakes' habits of crawling along perimeters of rooms rather than braving the open spaces. You can make one from a 2–3 foot (61–91 cm) section of plastic PVC pipe. Curl two pieces of heavy paper into two 6-inch-long (15 cm) cones, each with a 1-inch-wide (2.5 cm) opening at the end. Tape the cones onto each pipe end with the funnel openings pointing inward. The device works on the same principal as a funnel trap for fish by tempting a roaming snake to wander into the dark retreat it offers when encountered along a wall. They usually can't find the opening again and sit there until you check it, which must be done every day.

Other keepers have used glue trap boards (made for rodents) or duct tape with the sticky side up to snare small snakes. Although effective, these methods often leave the snake hopelessly mired, sometimes with damaged skin or jaws from twisting to escape.

Keep a close eye on the household cats or dogs. Their keen sense of smell and hearing may allow them to discover your lost pet before any human could. Unless supervised, they may "play" with their discovery and damage or kill the snake before it can be rescued from them.

Number of Snakes per Enclosure

Housing corns individually, except of course during breeding efforts, is the time-honored method for observation. This is especially important during the first few months of life. Separation ensures getting to know the personality quirks of each specimen in your care so you are able to make suitable husbandry adjustments for their individual needs.

You can also keep track of shedding and other life functions when you don't have to guess which of multiple cage inhabitants is responsible for leaving each clue. Just because they apparently enjoy "snuggling" up together when multiple snakes are temporarily housed together, it doesn't mean companionship is necessary for them to be comfortable. Rather than inferring they're combating loneliness, it's really a case of the snakes ending up sharing the same best spot offering shelter. Even just entwining in each other's coils is preferable to lying exposed in the open when no other hiding option exists.

If two (or more) cage mates cohabitate, you must closely monitor feeding to eliminate competition over single food items. If fed together, two hungry snakes will almost invariably seize the same prey, even with multiple choices in front of their noses. As they engulf the prey from each end, the snake whose bite first covers the snout of the other may continue to swallow its cage mate. The extremely rare instances of cannibalism in captive corns can usually be traced to this phenomenon.

Other times, one corn of a pair may be shy and intimidated, becoming a poor or sporadic feeder when faced with the fiercer competition of an aggressive cage mate. Using a temporary shift cage, which can be as simple as a clean empty garbage can, is a handy way to separate a pair of corns that otherwise live together in harmony during feeding. Gently lift the snake that usually grabs the food item first and put it into the can, since it's probably the more adventurous and less distracted feeder of the pair. There it can eat in peace while also reducing the risk of it, or any specimen prone to such tendencies, accidentally swallowing any loose cage substrate materials. Watch out when reintroducing it to its cage mate since the residual aroma of the prey on one snake's body could elicit a feeding strike from the other. Wait at least one half hour before reintroducing cage mates after a feeding frenzy.

If you feel you must keep two corns in the same cage, at least keep both separate for a minimum of their first three months in your care. This is a quarantine and acclimation time for them and an observation time for you. Putting them together immediately upon arrival at your facility increases the stress level for them at exactly the time they don't need more stress. It also denies you the time to get to know them as individuals before their personalities or habits change when faced with a new cage mate. If one corn does come down with anything contagious, it is likely that its cage mate will be infected as well.

Keeping a young pair of a male and female together at the onset of sexual maturity almost guarantees that the female will become gravid before she is ready size wise to bear that burden. Every spring we receive worried calls and emails from owners who assumed that their young pair of corns would not breed because they were not cooled or cycled in any way. They are faced with an unexpected clutch of eggs and a barely mature female with an increased risk of egg binding or other health problems. These potential problems can be avoided by housing your corns singly to lead a solitary lifestyle as they would in nature.

Cage Substrates

A good cage substrate should (1) absorb fecal material and stop it from spreading very far, (2) cover the cage floor to give the snake traction for movement, and (3) be visually appealing. Newspaper will work, but it tends to get folded over as the snake explores and defecates beneath it. Newspaper isn't pretty, but it's cheap and easy to change when soiled. Indoor-outdoor carpeting looks a little better but traps moisture below it, causing smells to linger and bacteria to grow. Snakes often hide under it and lie in wet filth unnoticed by their keepers for too long. Precut pieces that fit your cage must be ready to replace soiled ones within a day. Carpet pieces take a long time to dry thoroughly after washing and disinfecting, another reason to have many replacements on hand.

Wood chips and wood fibers are the substrates of choice in the United States today. A substrate material should cover the tank floor to a depth of 1–2 inches (2.5–5 cm). Some breeders prefer tiny granules of hard wood known as Sani-Chips. Aspen bedding is an alternative choice, consisting of a pale, shredded wood fiber with little dust or scent that works particularly well for this. It's absorbent, holding the solid and liquid portions of feces concentrated for easy removal. Aspen's interwoven nature also allows corns to tunnel through it while exploring, providing them hiding places in the "caves" formed under it. This is especially helpful for shy specimens that like to stay out of sight.

Cypress mulch (commonly used in gardening in the South) also works well because it shares many of the properties of aspen. However, not all kinds of similar mulch are good for reptiles. Avoid using resinous wood mulches such as cedar, pine, fir, and walnut, which have toxic aromas or oils especially dangerous to juveniles or animals in cages with low ventilation. Beddings made from the barks of these trees are to be particularly avoided. Logic dictates that the trees' natural insect-repelling chemicals would be concentrated in exposed bark more than in any other part of the tree. Breathing the vapors, drinking water that may have bark particles fallen into it, and having close physical contact with such materials year after year have caused problems to some herps.

Shelters and Hide Boxes

Corn snakes are shy by nature, spending the vast majority of their time tucked out of sight in tree holes and crevices, animal burrows, under debris, or in the walls and roofs of old buildings. This is a clue that providing a similar place of concealment in your snakes' enclosure is essential for their psychological health. Ideal hiding places allow snakes' entire bodies inside but are not large enough for an additional snake of the same size to fit inside, too. Juvenile corns are especially secretive, needing the security of snug places in which to hide to thrive. Don't be surprised if your new baby corn, after thoroughly examining the cage for escape routes, decides to spend most of its days and much of the nights secreted away in its retreat. It will probably become more confident and remain in the open more often once it has gained some size and maturity.

Corns like to squeeze into tight, dark places in order to feel secure from predators when they're digesting food, in shedding cycles, gravid, or just resting. A piece of wrinkled newspaper may suffice, although a shelter that's heavy enough to stay immobilized so it doesn't slide or tip over is often preferable. When a suitable choice is offered, your snake may spend the vast majority of its time comfortably concealed. If you weren't already aware of it, corn snakes lead rather boring lives by human standards. They rarely leave their lairs to prowl on display to the whole world except for particular reasons such as hunger and seeking mates.

Many common containers can serve as hide boxes as long as you make an opening in the container that's a little bigger around than the thickest part of the resident snake's body when distended by a meal. Margarine tubs, cardboard boxes, hollow or concave pieces of wood, or any number of creative custom products manufactured specifically for this purpose will work. Designs made of plastic are easier to clean than paper or wood, but cardboard boxes are free and disposable when soiled. If rock piles are chosen, be careful to stack them securely so they can't topple and pin or crush a pet accidentally.

Hanging the hide box from a wall or ceiling additionally keeps it up off the substrate to make removing feces from the cage floor simpler. Corns like to seek shelter in high places, so it's natural for them to utilize hiding places above ground level. A long, slender shelter, such as a hollow log sliced in half lengthwise, can provide the added bonus of a temperature range by extending across a portion of the cage

Three basic items needed in all cages are 1. a substrate such as wood chips, 2. a small but heavy water bowl, and 3. a place for the occupant to hide and feel secure.

under a heat lamp or over a heat tape or pad. This lets the snake avoid stress by being able to choose its preferred digestion temperature without having to bask in the open with a meal distending its stomach. Two identical hiding places, one at each end of the cage in different temperature zones, may also achieve this advantage while not forcing the snake to choose between its favorite hide box design and its favored temperature range.

Shedding

Snakes periodically shed (molt, slough) their skins, replacing the old, less flexible outer layer with a newer, cleaner, and more elastic layer of skin as they grow. Corns shed sooner and more often in response to skin injuries, speeding up the healing process over that given time period. The shedding process is technically known as ecdysis. In healthy corns, shedding occurs in one complete piece with every detail of its owner's scalation intact on the moist, flimsy white "stocking" of discarded skin. Discarded skins are left where they are shed, drying within hours to a more brittle texture that decomposes after only a couple of months when exposed to sun and rain.

The part of ecdysis that we can witness externally on the snake takes about seven to ten days from start to finish. One day the colors suddenly appear much duller than usual. Within a day or two, the snake's eyes cloud over with a milky

A corn snake in the blue-eyed or opaque state will be shedding its skin in approximately four to ten days. Note the dull lackluster appearance of its colors during this period. Even normally docile snakes may be slightly more nervous at this time.

or bluish cast. This condition persists for several more days and then disappears, leaving the eyes looking normally colored for an additional several days prior to the actual molting. Snakes become more shy and reclusive than usual during this period, and their normally calm attitude may temporarily be replaced by nervousness or readiness to nip your hand. Their appetites wane, too, but reappear with a vengeance as soon as the old skins are discarded.

Make sure that your corn snake's cage environment is conducive to shedding. A corn snake will have an easier time shedding if the humidity is heightened in the few days prior to the act. Misting the cage and substrate can help raise the ambient humidity in the cage. Laying a solid sheet of paper or plastic loosely over ventilated areas of the cage will help hold it in temporarily. The best solution, though, is adding a shedding box, a plastic tub with an entrance hole and containing damp moss or paper that the corn can pack itself into. Offering this option during the several days after the snake's eyes have cleared prior to shedding virtually always assures a clean, one-piece shed.

When it's time to shed, a corn will actively explore its cage, constantly rubbing its snout against walls, substrate, and any cage furniture encountered in an attempt to loosen the old skin from its nose and chin. Once started, it crawls forward to work the skin off, like peeling a tight stocking off your foot. If all goes well, the skin rolls off inside out in one continuous piece, with the tail of the shed pointing in the direction the snake traveled. This might be handy to know when a recently cast skin is discovered in the field and you're wondering which way the former occupant went.

A freshly shed skin is pliable, feels moist to the touch, and should even contain the clear spectacles that covered the eyes and every scale down to the tail tip. If the humidity is too low, or if the corn has suffered from skin irritations or poor diet, it can cause the skin to peel off in numerous ragged pieces. Sometimes scattered areas are left on the body where old, dry skin sticks fast. If patches like that remain on the body, they should be removed manually to avoid bacteria gaining a foothold by growing under the layers.

First try the easy route of leaving the snake overnight in a sack full of wet crumpled newspapers or rags (or secure it in its shedding box with the entrance hole blocked) so it can crawl through them and possibly loosen the old skin by itself. If this fails, soak the snake in water for at least fifteen minutes to soften the problem areas. Then sandwich the snake between some rough towels and let it force its way through them as you apply slight pressure. This usually lets the towel rub the problem areas and pull them free. Be sure to notice that every inch of old skin is removed right down to the tail tip. That's where an accumulation of old dry skin can restrict blood flow and eventually kill the tail tissue, causing it to slough off and leave a slightly stubbed tip.

After dealing with the shedding problem, the keeper should be alert to observe the beginning of the next shed cycle. At that time, a shedding box can be offered as soon as the snake's eyes cloud over and "go blue," thus avoiding a repetition of the ordeal. Never start peeling a snake that you feel has gone too long before shedding—premature manual shedding invites infection and can be a death sentence to a snake. Unless you're 100 percent sure the snake can't initiate the process at all, wait until the difficult shed starts coming off by itself before trying to "help."

If either eye cap or spectacle—the clear covering over each cornea that's part of the snake's skin—does not appear intact in the sloughed head portion of the skin, it may create a place for an infection to start. For this reason, most keepers opt to remove eye caps manually. First use a wet sponge to swab the eyes to soften them a little, but avoid the use of glycerin or any other skin-softening product intended for humans. Then try rubbing your thumb over the eye in an attempt to partially dislodge an edge of the stuck cap. We've found that tweezers with pointy tips are the handiest tool to get a hold of the extra skin covering that often protrudes in places at the edge of the eye. Gently fish around for a solid grip on the edge of the eye cap, slide a tip under it, and simply lift it away. This sounds difficult and may make you squeamish, but the tough spectacles of serpents' eyes are not nearly as sensitive to slight bumping or as easily injured as those of humans. On the other hand, extreme caution must be taken to be sure that only the extra cap is grasped with the tweezers and not the cornea itself.

A word of reassurance—don't fret if you're not ready to tackle this kind of operation. We've rarely seen a single stuck eye cap actually develop into a serious problem. The easiest, safest route is to just wait for the caps to come off with the next molt, which they nearly always do. You can facilitate that likelihood by leaving a hide box, half full of damp moss or paper towels, in the cage when the snake's eyes next cloud over prior to shedding.

Water and Humidity

Because corns inhabit the relatively humid southeastern United States, they have higher moisture requirements than comparably sized desert species such as western gopher snakes (genus *Pituophis*). The lower relative humidity inside typical homes everywhere may cause incomplete shedding or dehydration problems that wouldn't be suspected at first. This can be a major problem for juvenile corn snakes in particular, since they are much more prone to desiccation than adults. In these cases, it may be necessary to provide a slightly more humid environment within the cage. This may be done by covering most of the main ventilation areas of the cage to reduce moisture loss by evaporation. Newspaper laid on top of a screen aquarium lid may be enough to do the trick, or you may need sheet plastic held down by tape, with only a few air holes, to hold water vapor in more thoroughly.

The amount of time a corn spends coiled inside its water bowl will help you evaluate the degree of discomfort it's experiencing with desiccation, overheating, shedding, or a mite infestation. Monitor for skin blisters more frequently than usual if your snake spends days on end in the water. A small, sturdy water bowl for drinking (3–6 inches [7.5–15 cm] in diameter) is all that's normally required by healthy corn snakes. A larger soaking pan can be added temporarily only if deemed necessary during difficulty in shedding. Placement of all water containers should be central in enclosures since most feces are deposited along cage perimeters where the snakes prowl most often. An exception may be made for new baby corns that may not find the water before becoming dehydrated. Water bowl placement on the cage perimeter will ensure that they find it quickly enough to prevent any problems.

Splurge and buy two identical water bowls that lack the outwardly flared rims that snakes can easily spill by lifting them with their coils. The solid types without hollow spaces underneath are heavier and stay in place best. The water and the bowl should be replaced at least every three days to prevent a buildup of harmful bacteria. Keep in mind that the water doesn't have to look dirty to be unhealthy! Set the newly removed and rinsed bowl upside down to dry while it's not in use. Periodically soak all bowls for at least ten minutes in a bleach-based or other strong antibacterial solution to prevent germs from accumulating on the surfaces.

Another way to increase humidity is to provide a shedding box in the snake's cage to create a moist retreat without raising the humidity of the entire cage. The down side of this arrangement is that some corns will spend too much time in the shedding box simply because it's darker and cozier than their other hide box. Blisters may develop from too much constant dampness against their bodies, and such damp conditions will promote growth of mold and bacteria. Check your snakes often, especially the ventral plates, for signs of sores or unusual redness if they seem to spend all their time in their shedding box. The safest compromise is to put the damp hiding place in the cage when a snake's eyes go blue before it sheds, and then to remove the dampness after the snake sheds. The damp material can be discarded and new damp material used in the next shed cycle.

The dryness of your climate will dictate your method and whether additional periodic misting with a spray bottle is necessary. Even living in a nonarid zone may present dryness-related problems if air conditioning or winter home heating tends to severely dehumidify the air where your corns are kept. The most obvious determinant of whether additional moisture is necessary is if your corn snake fails to shed its skin in one long piece, including the eye caps.

Live Plant Usage

To turn a basic terrarium into a truly beautiful display vivarium for your home, you can decorate it with live plants to add a natural element. Their dash of greenery throws life into an otherwise drab setting of only logs and stones. Sturdy plants that can resist the flattening effect of being repeatedly crawled over are recommended. Also, species that thrive in low-light indoor situations work best because cage lighting rarely offers the intensity or full spectrum many plants need to grow properly.

Pothos species is a spreading vine that may be grown directly in the enclosure and allowed to spread since it's hardy enough to survive in most home environments. For continued health, rotate them regularly with stand-ins so the plants receive some natural light during the times in between being on active display inside cages. Aloes, bromeliads, and snake plants (*Sansevieria* species) are durable types that can, better than most, withstand repeatedly being crawled over by adult corns. Keep them potted and away from cage perimeters and corners to avoid crushing by wandering or hiding snakes.

Maintaining live plants is more work than using artificial plants due to having to water them and risking adding too much moisture to cage substrates if it seeps beyond the plants' vicinity. The moistened soil may also harbor germs or parasites, considerations to make when deciding how naturalistic an exhibit to create for your corn snakes. For these reasons, few American herpeticulturists keep live plants in with their corn snakes.

Heating

Corns thrive at temperatures in the same range that humans find to be comfortable. This means approximately a range of 70°F–88°F (21°C–31°C). But unlike humans with self-regulating body temperatures, snakes can't sustain all bodily functions if kept at a constant temperature. There are times when they must experience higher or lower temperatures to facilitate natural functions such as digestion, embryo development, parasite or infection control, or spermatogenesis. Thermoregulation is the freedom of choice process by which herps purposely move in and out of areas of higher or lower heat to optimize their body temperatures for various functions.

In nature, the sun is the ultimate source of heat, either directly (basking) or indirectly (by warming other surfaces upon which snakes rest). Snakes seek warmth from those options when they know they need it. Basking in sunlight is by far the method corn snakes use most often. They can count on the sun on most days of the year in the wild range. Denying this vital freedom to them is surely an important factor behind many of the health problems that arise in the often-restrictive, constant environments that many keepers provide for their pets in captivity.

A good method of offering heat to a limited portion of a cage is through a heating device under or inside one end of it. Heating pads (used for aching backs) can work in a pinch if slid under one end of a cage. They may not be waterproof though, so don't use them inside the cage where they might be defecated upon and shorted out. Don't use the adhesive strips offered on some models because they tend to become glued on permanently to your cage bottom and can't easily be moved to other cages. Instead, use duct tape to attach them until you wish to move them to another cage. Be sure that the heating pad does not cover the entire cage bottom, denying the corn a chance to escape the heat when needed.

You can buy heat tapes that are normally used for warming the soil to help seeds germinate early or to wrap around outdoor water pipes in northern climates to prevent them from freezing. In the past, herpers typically ran a length of heat tape along the rear edge of a shelf so many cages would benefit from hot spots where the end of each enclosure rested over it. The thermostats that are usually built into such units are useless because they only turn the heat on when the temperature gets down to near freezing.

All models we've seen work better with the factory thermostat, if present, disengaged. A separate thermostat that reacts to less severe lows is then rigged up , rather than left to heat constantly day and night.

Modern herpetoculturists' lives have been made much easier by new thermostat control units made especially for herps' needs. Excellent units that can accurately monitor and regulate any kind of temperature-altering electrical device are available today, taking much of the guesswork out of the situation. These devices, combined with slender heat pads or tapes that barely take up space anchored beneath cage bottoms or under the interior substrate, have greatly simplified and reduced the fire and shock risks of providing heat. Again, check the herp magazine ads for models and sources.

Hot rocks use electrical wires inside a molded form to provide a distinct warm point to warm herps' bellies when they lie on them. They can be best used for corns if the rock is under a larger than usual hide box that covers a floor space equivalent to at least three times the area of the rock. That way, the corn can be hidden while absorbing warmth, yet have enough room to avoid the heat if it becomes excessive while still remaining out of sight. The point is to avoid forcing the snake to choose between heat and shelter. In our own facility, we have always preferred heat sources that do not require electrical cords inside the cage.

Spotlights or hooded reflectors may also be used to direct incandescent light to a special basking rock or branch that the snake can utilize easily. Be sure that such a source of radiant heat is aimed at only one end of the cage so a cooler and darker retreat exists at the far end. The basking temperature on the perch site directly under the lamp should be in the 90s°F (over 32°C). This slightly "too hot" spot allows the snake to thermoregulate properly to reach the temperatures it desires or needs, but also lets it move away from it when warm enough, just as it would do in sunlight. The light should shine through a metal mesh cage top or side vent so the snake can't crawl directly on the bulb and possibly get stuck against it and be burned.

Lighting

Besides lights for heat, you may wish to illuminate the entire enclosure in a tone of light that beautifies the interior and the inhabitant(s). Corn snakes' colors look best in daylight with only the sun providing the light. Diffused lighting on cloudy days actually makes their colors appear even more vibrant than when exposed to bright, direct sunlight. Daylight-simulating (or enhancing) fluorescent bulbs that have brightened fish aquariums for years also make corn snakes look beautiful and sometimes more fluorescent than in natural light.

Some brands of fluorescent bulbs advertise that they give off limited amounts of ultraviolet (UV) light that benefits many life-forms. The UV light they emit is known to be important for some lizards and turtles but seems inconsequential to healthy snakes' well-being as far as has been determined at this time. But it doesn't seem to hurt them either. It could be of benefit to sick animals if they're able to get very close—24 inches (61 cm) or less—to it.

Incandescent bulbs tend to give off a yellowish light, although some types are less yellow than others. The GE Reveal bulb may give more pleasing results than many other incandescent choices. Halogen lighting is whiter. It gives off warmth and won't harm corns, but it alters their colors by washing out the reds and oranges somewhat. Based on current information, our best advice is for you to use whichever brand or style of light that fits your needs best and produces the most eye-pleasing results in your display. Acquiring bulbs with the highest color rendering index (CRI) value obtainable will promote the most natural colors on your animals.

Joseph Laszlo, a pioneer herp breeder in the zoo world whose early experiments with Vita-Lites were pivotal in herpetocultural progress, felt that herps act more naturally when the color spectrum of light they live under closely mimics the sun. We concur that this makes them happier, and we strive to make the maximum use of the sun's lighting whenever feasible. The obviously elite choice is allowing unfiltered sunlight to bathe your snake's cage for both a warm basking site and best color rendition, as long as a significant portion is shaded to prevent heat buildup from a miniature greenhouse effect within the cage. Barring the ability to do this, using nontinted skylights in your herp room is an admirable next-best option. Clear diffusers hanging just below skylights can help spread sunlight over the room while also preventing it from shining directly onto any cage and baking it.

Artificial cage lights for all captive reptiles are most easily (and regularly) controlled with a simple electrical timer. Daylight length per day in the northernmost range of wild corn snakes (in south-central New Jersey) ranges from as low as about nine hours at the winter solstice (December 21 in the northern hemisphere) to a high of fifteen and a half hours at the summer solstice on June 21. This equates to a daily lengthening of just over two minutes per day from late December through late June. In southern Florida, at the southern end of their range, the equivalent range is more like eleven to fourteen and a half hours, or just over one minute per day. You should approximate these times in captivity. Resetting the timer daily is unnecessary; adding fifteen to thirty minutes every couple of weeks is fine. The reverse is true during the shortening half of the year, of course.

Corn snakes, and all herps for that matter, never live with lights on twenty four hours per day in the wild. It's stressful and disruptive to their biological clocks to live under constant lights-on conditions in captivity. The simplest plans are to turn all cage lights off for the same hours each day that you are asleep or get an inexpensive, basic electric timer to run the lights twelve hours on, twelve hours off as a basic daily plan. Don't be tempted to leave a light on for warmth; it will not be too cold for your corn snake in the same room in which you spend the night. If letting your snake digest a large meal in a cold room is a concern, either feed lighter, smaller meals, or invest in a small, undertank heating pad as well.

Altering the time your cage lights are on daily during the course of a year is one of the keys to stimulate breeding. More on this later.

CHAPTER 4

FEEDING

Corn snakes are strict carnivores, capturing and swallowing whole food animals in the wild. Struggling prey is subdued by constriction, a process by which coils of the snake's body are wrapped around the animal in ever-tightening loops until inhalation, heartbeats, and circulation become impossible. Death usually occurs within two minutes for mammals and birds, occasionally slightly longer for cold-blooded prey.

Corn snakes are "stretchier" than milk and king snakes (*Lampropeltis* species), but they are less able to swallow huge meals than boas, pythons, and even their rat snake relatives of the species *E. obsoleta*. It's easy to understand that a corn snake lucky enough to find an adult rat or bird in a tree on any given evening's foray could not afford to pass it by, even if it were bigger than the snake might prefer to capture and swallow. This logically means that being physically geared for handling large single food lumps would be a wise strategy. Yet corns are semiterrestrial in habit, so an occasional discovery of a nest of multiple baby rodents or birds is also a distinct likelihood. In such circumstances, corn snakes are fully prepared to gorge themselves on the entire brood, knowing they can optimize the digestion of an unusually big meal with careful thermoregulation over the next few days.

Corn snakes seek out different foods, depending on their size. Juvenile corns readily accept tree frogs, small lizards such as anoles and house geckos, and newborn rodents, among other things. Crickets and other insects are not part of corn snakes' diets, even if a novice pet shop employee recommends buying them as food. Adult specimens more than 3 feet (0.9 m) in length feed almost exclusively on warm-blooded prey such as fully furred rodents and birds in the wild. Food items are normally sought during evenings and at night, though corns may be active at any hour of the day or night when weather conditions are favorable. The norm is for them to consume large meals relative to their body size and then conceal themselves for several days to a week while digestion takes place. The first defecation from the most recent meal comes two to four days after eating, depending on temperature. At that point, the snake is often interested in eating again, though not always. It's not necessary to feed large corns immediately after they defecate; in nature they might easily spend the next week in search of food items, receiving plenty of exercise in the process.

Feeding Schedule for Adults and Hatchlings

We estimate that a very average feeding schedule in captivity for older corns—those 3–4 feet (91–122 cm) or longer—might be one or two appropriate-sized food animals every seven to fourteen days. One old adult (retired breeder) mouse, two young subadult mice, or one barely weaned rat makes a perfect single meal for an average adult 4–5 foot-long (137–152 cm) corn snake. The rule of thumb we use to gauge correct size of food animals is to try to select food items (ignoring the prey's fur or feather fluffiness in the estimate) that don't exceed one and one-half times the girth of the snake at midbody. A corn can handle larger prey if all other aspects of the cage environment are ideally suited to let the snake find its preferred temperature and digest its food efficiently. Because of the greater surface area to mass ratio of small items, it's often wiser to give two or more small food items rather than one, huge, hard-to-digest one. Providing a hot spot in the cage so snakes can choose their optimum digestion temperature on a free-will basis takes the guesswork away from you and puts it into the "hands" of the real experts—the snakes themselves.

Newly hatched corns need and want to eat more often than adults. Baby corns usually possess fat reserves to carry

Meals distending a corn snake's profile any more than depicted here are stressful to the snake and risk regurgitation if digestion conditions aren't perfect.

them through the initial month of life in good condition even if no other source of food is encountered. A small percentage of hatchlings will accept food within days of emerging from their eggs, but the vast majority will wait the approximate week until they shed their skins for the first time. After the postnatal shed, a baby corn is ready to be offered food, which, out of convenience for pet keepers, is typically a single pinkie (one that's fewer than five days old) mouse, not rat. A pinkie mouse is enough of a meal for a 10 to 12-inch (25–30 cm) youngster. Just lay the mouse in the cage near wherever the snake is presently hiding, preferably without disturbing the snake in the process. Do not drop it on top of a snake or place it inside the hide box because this may frighten the snake by its sudden too-close proximity. Under ideal digestive conditions—those in which the snake can warm up to 90°F (32°C) over or under a hot spot at its own discretion—complete digestion will occur in two to three days. After that initial meal has passed through the snake's digestive system and the remains have been defecated in a healthy stool (usually two to three days later), additional pinkies may be offered, one or two at a time, every three to ten days. Offer pinkies one at a time so as not to frighten or confuse the snake with multiple squirming food items.

Giving more than two food items at one time will sometimes result in overloading baby snakes' stomachs beyond their ability to easily digest such elongated loads. If the snake regurgitates an oversized food item (one greater than about one and one half times the diameter of its girth at midbody) or a multiple item meal, go back to offering only one very small food item per meal for a few weeks. Then work up to larger meals again slowly if no further digestive problems are encountered. As a general rule, it is better to offer smaller meals more often than to maximize the size of each one.

Avoid prolonged exposure to unvarying temperatures less than about 72°F (22°C) and more than 90°F (32°C) for snakes of any age, because regurgitation of undigested food items often results. Minimize disturbances to snakes with food bulges in their stomachs until the first main feces appear in the cage. This is especially true when more than two food items are eaten or when an exceptionally large meal distends the snake's profile to over one and one-half times its normal diameter anywhere along its length. Corns usually stay hidden at such times to avoid the stress of contact with potential danger. A good general rule of thumb is to let all snakes rest—no handling or bothering them in any way—for three days after any meal!

Corn snakes are best offered rodents that are approximately 1 to 1.5 times the diameter of the thickest part of their body. This specimen is engulfing a mouse that's at the upper end of the suitable size range for a single meal.

Feeding Behavior

Ideal temperature conditions for corns to hunt and feed are typically from the mid 70s°F to high 80s°F (roughly 24°C–31°C). An hour before and after dusk with moderate to high humidity is a favored activity time, which is one more variable to consider when faced with a stubborn feeder in captivity. A hungry corn may slowly wander out of its resting abode and actively flick its tongue repeatedly at any time of day. The Jacobson's organ in the roof of its mouth analyzes minute airborne particles from the forked tongue tips while also determining direction of the strongest or most desirable scent. Accumulated chemical cues help the snake zero in on potential prey while approaching within its preferred striking distance of less than 8 inches (20 cm).

A snake performs an open-mouthed lunge to sink its teeth into the intended prey to pull the animal backward toward itself, or to anchor the snake so it can pull itself forward to engage its coils. The fore portion of the prey, especially the head or shoulder region, is often targeted in the strike. Presumably this allows better control of the struggling victim's mouth, which in the case of an adult rodent or bird may be a dangerous weapon capable of injuring the snake. The objective is then rapid immobilization by constriction. That killing method works via a combination of suffocation and vascular compression; victims' bones and organs are not actually "crushed."

When all movement of the prey ceases, the snake releases its grip so it can seek the prey's head, where the swallowing process virtually always begins. The snake uses a combination of tactile cues from the overlap direction of the hair or feathers and rapid tongue flicks to find the best starting point. The gradually widening contour commencing at the narrow snout end of prey animals, combined with the lay of the hair or feathers, lends itself to the slow engulfing process more readily than when swallowing food backwards. Breech feeding also is not unusual and rarely causes any difficulty unless the meal is extremely large; it typically just takes a little longer, from a couple of minutes to twenty minutes or more. All snakes are best left undisturbed during swallowing, when they feel vulnerable to attack and it is very likely that they may spit out their food item if nervous.

Rodent Bites to Snakes

Injuries resulting from live rodents bites are a rare occurrence because corn snakes are very adept at subduing such prey when they're hungry. Problems happen most often when live adult rodents are left in a snake's cage for many hours, especially overnight. If the snake is disinterested in feeding for any reason, incredibly it may allow a hungry or thirsty rodent to literally chew off its skin and flesh while lying in the cage seemingly unaware. The way to prevent this is quite simple—don't leave such potentially dangerous rodents in with your corns unattended. When you can't keep a constant eye on the situation inside the cage, at least leave some food like a slice of fruit and piece of bread or a nut for the mouse or rat to nibble on. This reduces, but doesn't absolutely eliminate, the risk. It's safe to leave rodents that haven't yet opened their eyes in cages with snakes, although it's possible for substrate material to cling to them and be ingested as snakes swallow them. There is always a slight but real risk of injury to your snake when feeding live rodents. You must evaluate the danger and decide for yourself if you wish to accept the degree of risk posed by each situation.

Frozen Rodents and Commercial Snake Diets

Domestically raised rodents have a reduced chance of passing diseases and parasites to humans or reptiles than do wild-caught prey items. Lab rodents address the nutritional needs of corn snakes admirably, largely due to the decades of exhaustive research behind formulation of the commercial laboratory chows used to conveniently feed and propagate most rodent colonies today. However, not all small-scale rodent breeders feed their rodents these nutritious large pellet diets. Some breeders opt for utilizing the cheapest dog foods and day-old bread that they can acquire to feed their mice and rats. Their cost cutting may result in vitamin-deficient food animals.

Choose a reputable source of rodents to meet your snakes' nutritional needs. Question your source of rodents thoroughly about the diet their stock is fed to better assess if your snakes' nutritional requirements will be met by using their animals. This may be of even greater pertinence if the rodents they sell are frozen for a long time prior to use because the value of many foods slowly declines during long periods of storage.

You can't beat the convenience that frozen diets provide. Frozen rodents come in every size and description. They can be purchased at most pet shops that cater to herp-oriented clientele or bought via mail order quite easily. Their greatest advantage is the convenience of having appropriate-sized meals handily stashed away in your home freezer for whenever they're needed. Most hobbyists prefer frozen rodents over live because of the convenience, lower cost resulting from buying in bulk, and because there is absolutely no risk of injury due to rodent bites.

The freezing process breaks down the food item's cell walls, inducing a stronger aroma to waft through the herp room as food thaws, stimulating snakes' appetites. The same effect also makes thawed food more easily digested so that somewhat larger meals can be safely offered and fully assimilated by specimens not currently in the peak of health. You can defrost the prey several ways. You can place the frozen prey in a plastic bag (to avoid washing away the rodents' natural scent) and soak the bag in warm water; leave the prey items out at normal room temperatures on a tray; or even quick-thaw them in a microwave oven at the defrost setting (not full power or they may explode) to prepare them for feeding to hungry corns. With the microwave method, watch out for hot spots on the ends of food items and unthawed middles on bulky morsels.

Freezing lizards and frogs (sometimes used as food for juveniles) also kills many pathogens and parasites that may be harbored inside those animals, which were probably captured in the wild. Most residential freezers do not reach cold enough temperatures to kill all bacteria, so refreezing of uneaten food items, especially for more than just a few days until the next feeding time, is not recommended.

Long-term frozen food storage results in the slow loss of nutrients. Our goal is to not hold frozen rodents in home freezers for more than a few months. The reality is that

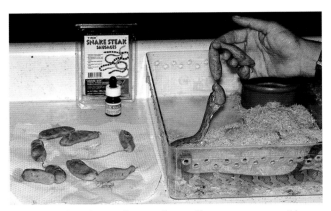

"Snake Steak Sausages" – little links of ground whole animals made in several sizes – provide the closest thing to replacing a diet of actual rodents.

we've used rodents frozen for well over a year with no adverse results noticed. Shrink-wrapping packs of frozen rodents may help combat that tendency.

The thawing preparation advice applies equally well to frozen Snake Steak Sausages by T-Rex. They are made from whole ground vertebrate carcasses, including all parts except fur, feathers, and intestines. They are cased in sausage skin units to take the place of actual rodents as herp food. The sausages are made in sizes ranging from those approximating newborn mice to medium-sized rats. They come in short connected chains resembling strings of hotdogs and sausages, making feeding multiple sections a cinch. A special Mouse Maker scenting fluid (Lizard Maker is also available) has even been devised to dab on the end of each link to impart the smell of mice and complete the deception. The concept is old, but the actual product is new in the booming herp pet trade. Snake Steak Sausages may be a welcome answer for those objecting to frozen mice sharing home freezer space with the family steaks.

We tested two of the four manufactured sausage sizes at our home because we were particularly interested to see how juvenile corns would respond. In a first-time test, a selected group of forty-seven voluntarily-feeding six-month-old corns were each offered one of the smallest sausages scented with Mouse Maker. A single link was left in each snake's shoe box for one hour. On the initial try, twenty-three of them accepted the sausage with little hesitation, and sixteen of the others took theirs during the following hour after we rubbed the rejected links with frozen mice. We were impressed that more than 75 percent of our young corns wolfed down the sausages on our first test evaluation. Subsequent tests with new hatchlings have shown (in our experience, at least) that it is more effective to get the hatchlings started on live or frozen pinkie mice first, rather than try to feed them sausages for their first few meals.

Jon Coote in England reports that tests spanning five years on breeding colonies of colubrids, two-thirds of which were corn snakes, yielded positive results raising to adulthood babies that were fed sausages for approximately 98 percent of their total dietary intake. Those same adults bred and produced healthy offspring, showing that the sausages appear capable of sustaining corns through their entire life cycle.

An additional advantage is that the sausages don't tend to bloat within snakes' stomachs like whole animals because the finely packed ground contents lack air pockets. Sausages are softer than baby mice and have a tendency to fall apart when thawed. Also, they must be cut apart into whatever size chains of links you need. We believe that most corn snakes can be trained to accept them, although it will probably take longer to train new hatchlings than larger feeders already well established on conventional food items.

Vitamin and Mineral Supplements

An overwhelming number of vitamin and mineral supplements is available on the market. They are largely intended to augment the more varied diets of omnivorous or strictly vegetarian herps that are difficult to duplicate in captivity. Even corn snakes benefit from extra nutrition found in food items' stomach contents, such as insects, seeds, and vegetation. Captive corn diets may be deficient in an assortment of nutrients, so we see no harm in periodic supplementation of food items with any of the finely powdered products advertised in herp magazines— as long as you don't supplement at every meal.

Many of the vitamins are water soluble, with excess amounts excreted quickly. Most don't easily build up to unnaturally toxic levels if given only sporadically, but a few of the fat-soluble vitamins may accumulate. Since there is no standard of minimum daily requirements established for corn snakes, the best strategy may be to give supplements only a few times per year. This would allow their bodies time to excrete excessive amounts if you unknowingly overdose them with any particular ingredient. This method would space the intake of trace elements at irregular intervals much as they'd get in the wild when odd meals bring them large doses unexpectedly. Dusting food items with calcium powder during the breeding season may be especially valuable to intensively bred female corns so that heavy egg production doesn't weaken them by drawing too much calcium from their skeletal systems.

Supplements are usually administered in one of several ways. The first approach is by dipping a food item into the product, which is either a fine powder or a liquid. Both types will stick to the prey animal's fur or skin. Dip only the rear end of a rodent because the strange new odor may confuse snakes if the head end that they normally seek first doesn't smell right. Secondly, you can inject the liquid version into live rodents with a syringe. A third strategy involves gut-loading the feeder animals while they're alive, a technique that has been used for years on insects for lizards and amphibians. You could gut-load rodents by mixing special heavy doses of the supplement into a watery gruel of their normal chow, allow it to dry into new enhanced food bricks, give it to hungry rodents just before feeding them to snakes. We'd suggest using rodents fed in this way within a few hours before any of the products are passed and lost.

Feeding Strategies

Wild corn snakes normally hunt for live prey items. Visual and chemosensory cues from potential food are both important clues aiding corns in finding and identifying prey. Most successful hunts rely on utilizing both senses. Detecting and following a scent trail is possible when the snake is a greater distance away from prey. This is what normally helps most in tracking down a meal. When closer, the prey's movement triggers the final lunge to grab it. In captivity, however, nearly all specimens can be induced to eat live prey items that smell right by simulating movement in the food item by dangling it on the end of a forceps.

Live Prey Versus Pre-Killed Food

A diet of live prey typically assures that the meals are fresh and nutritious. Corn snakes engage in considerable physical effort seeking, immobilizing, and ingesting living prey while also risking injury in the killing process from bites and scratches from struggling rodents and birds. Conversely, offering only pre-killed food in captivity eliminates the chance of injury from resisting food items but also minimizes the exercise they receive in finding and subduing their food. However, if the keeper carefully manipulates the thawed food to simulate live prey, the snake will use almost as much energy as if the food was live prey.

Not every wild-caught corn will accept food in captivity, and even some captive-bred individuals balk at food differing slightly from what they're used to. Be prepared for several attempts at inducing a new corn to eat voluntarily, using every trick at your disposal. First, try offering food just after dark when corns are normally beginning their daily hunting cycle. Try every possible combination of variably sized prey, live *versus* dead, fresh-killed *versus* thawed frozen, and different kinds of prey. Various species of prey have distinctive smells and palatabilities to snakes, so try rats, hamsters, gerbils, day-old chicks, or any type of odd rodent you can find. Wild deer mice and white-footed mice of the genus *Peromyscus* are found throughout the natural range of corn snakes and are sometimes the keys to getting a fussy corn's attention when all else fails.

Stimulating with Scent

When dealing with stubborn feeders, we have found that a significant number of corn snakes will eat pinkie mice after the mice have been lightly buried in the dirty shavings of deer mice or other rodents in order to absorb the new odor. Possibly a pet shop or breeder may be able to supply dirty bedding from several different rodent species to be tried out as scenting materials at different times.

Introduce the food, only one item at a time, with minimal jarring of the cage so the snake isn't overly spooked by the intrusion. Leave the item a few inches in front of the entrance hole to the snake's hiding place. Do not touch the snake's body or head with the food—this will only scare a nervous captive. Get out of the room so peace and quiet reign, and don't come back for at least ten minutes so the shyest snake can eat undisturbed. Don't turn the light on when you do return to check; if necessary, use a small flashlight to view the cage, avoiding shining it at the snake's head.

If that doesn't work, next in the arsenal of methods is offering food from tweezers, forceps, or tongs. These tools' slender profiles don't frighten snakes like a thick arm and hand in front of their snouts. We've found 18-inch (46 cm) scissors-style stainless steel hemostat forceps the handiest to maneuver. Mechanical finger devices sold at auto parts stores also work well. With a dead rodent held at the tip, approach the corn from a low angle (high angle approaches are more threatening to the snake) to let it see and smell the item. Keep very still so you don't distract it with any motions from your own body—you want its total attention riveted to the object in front of it. Slowly move it around the vicinity of the snake's head, at the same time studying the snake's reaction. The trick is to not appear intimidating while tempting the snake to strike a small, unthreatening helpless item.

If the snake advances toward the item, back the prey away to gently induce the snake to give chase. Move the food farther away to draw the snake out of its lair until it feels confident enough to attack. When it does grab the food item, cease all movement—don't even breathe—while it constricts the prey and hopefully follows through and eats the food.

If the snake is out of its shelter, you can sometimes stimulate interest in the prey item by gently touching or stroking the snake's midbody with the rodent held in the forceps. Avoid direct contact with the snake's head because it interprets this as a frontal attack, causing it to respond in fear or anger. You want instead to elicit curiosity and a feeding strike. Again try the teasing action to get the snake to follow the rodent after it turns to face the prey, pausing when it seems ready to pounce. Keep the rodent's nose low and pointing forward at all times so the snake will be more likely to grab it by the head. Be slow and patient, and be ready to freeze once the bait is taken. Be alert in noting a snake's responses to your varied movements so you can refine your method through trial and error.

Feeding is about the only time that corns act in what could be deemed an aggressive manner. Corns quickly learn to associate the opening of their cage and a hand entering as a signal to grab food before it escapes. If your corns have an excitable feeding response, offer dead food items with forceps, large tweezers, or tongs to avoid bites by the corns. Using a long, slender, less-noticeable instrument for offering food helps break the association between your hand and food so that attempts to simply handle the snake are not always met with an open-mouthed charge. Another calming strategy is to first lift the snake out of its home cage with a snake hook and place it in a second empty container, such as a large plastic garbage can. This helps to train it that feeding always takes place in a separate feeding cage. This extra effort soon pays off when a corn is an unusually volatile feeder or if it's expected to be handled often, especially by children. Most corns are not excitable enough to require these extra precautions.

Use caution during feeding so excited corns don't strike wildly and injure themselves on instruments, cage walls, furniture, and cage mates. You also don't want them to end up with a mouthful of cage substrate if they miss the meal when they lunge. Their fervor doesn't always stop after the first food morsel either. We've often seen corns enter a sort of feeding frenzy immediately after the first item is barely down their gullets, quickly grabbing anything nearby that moves or that is even bumped into. Be ready to take advantage of this behavior by having the next piece of food close at hand so it's what the snake sees first.

Increasing Meal Size

There may be times when you wish to try to achieve maximum growth in your corn snake or build its weight up quickly again after sickness or laying a huge clutch of eggs. Offering multiple food items is one way of accomplishing this. If your time or patience is at a minimum, use the simple "dump it and run" method of just placing additional prey items in the cage near the action. This way the snake will eagerly seek and devour the second and third food items after finishing the first. A piece of newspaper or small paper plate left underneath the food helps minimize the amount of substrate material that clings to the food and thus accidentally ingested. Such debris usually passes through corns' digestive tracts without incident. Occasionally, though, it can cause impactions or lacerations in the gut, especially if small snakes swallow large or sharp pieces of woody or fibrous material.

Corns seem to stay interested in eating for only ten to fifteen minutes per instance of feeding. If no new opportunities come along within that amount of time after the initial item is consumed, they usually lose interest and settle back into their favorite retreat, showing no further desire to eat. For this reason, plan on all feeding sessions concluding within that time range. Unlike turtles and some lizards that eat almost continuously throughout the day as food becomes available, with corn snakes you usually can't get away with returning every half hour to offer an additional rodent between sessions of watching TV.

With a greater investment of time and effort, you can use a technique called chain feeding to increase the size of each meal by increasing the number of food items per meal. Carefully ease a second food item between the snake's jaws as it's finishing the first. It will often continue engulfing the extra-long meal without noticing the deception if you place the prey in with a gentle touch. The connected links of Snake Steak Sausages are particularly handy for chain feeding.

Chain feeding is rarely necessary with hardy corn snakes, but it's quite handy for giving medicines or other supplements stuffed inside a second meal that you want to be certain is ingested. Sometimes such additive materials exude a disagreeable odor that snakes will avoid if left to examine at their leisure, as they might with the first item. They'll often engulf a second item containing the materials in the excitement of the initial feeding frenzy when no pause comes in a chain of food items going down their throats.

We always try to avoid touching food items any more than is necessary so their natural smell is not removed or masked by our own. This is particularly important when handling pinkies, which do not possess the powerful attractant scent of mature rodents. We keep pinkies and fuzzies in a tray with aromatic bin bedding from the adult rodents' cages until they're fed to the snakes. The pungent aroma of the tray also acts as an enticing announcement that the opportunity to feed is near if you leave the pans of food items in your snakes' vicinity for fifteen minutes in advance. The dinner fragrance will waft across the room and heighten your corns' anticipation levels.

Coaxing Stubborn Hatchlings to Feed

Most hatchling corn snakes produced for today's market recognize pinkie mice as food. Keep in mind that lizards and frogs are also normal, if not preferred, starter food items of hatchling corns in the wild. The emphasis we've put on getting them to recognize and eat baby mice is based upon convenience for keepers. There's nothing wrong with offering them their natural foods (if those kinds of items are available to you) at the beginning of their lives to start them off with less stress. Freezing those cold-blooded animals (a fast, humane technique to kill cold-blooded food animals) prior to using them will largely eliminate the threat of parasite transfer. The other threat is contamination from pesticides or toxic chemicals that may have been accumulated by wild frogs and lizards through diet or impure ground water. We recommend avoiding the use of any kind of prey captured in the wild except as a last resort.

The first thing to remember is that normal, healthy babies come into the world with a good-sized meal in their bellies in the form of the egg yolk that was absorbed in the last few hours before exiting the egg. Some babies will eat in their first week of life, but most will wait until their first shed at about one week of age. They then have about one month or so before it becomes critical that another meal is consumed. Relax—you have some time to work on them!

During the first month of trial feedings, avoid constantly harassing your neonate with daily attempts at feeding—you will just stress out both the snake and yourself! Try the various methods listed below about every three or four days and don't bother the baby between feeding attempts. After a month or more has passed (or just a few weeks if your corn was hatched prematurely and did not absorb the yolk), it is time to move on to the "last resort" methods outlined below.

If you have a difficult feeder, a number of tricks may help you persuade it to accept baby mice. The first is to be sure that it's housed alone in a comfortable cage environment as described earlier, one that's not so large that the food gets lost in the wide-open spaces and is never found by the snake. Be sure your corn has found the water and is well-hydrated before attempting to feed. The temperature should be in the mid-80s °F (28–31 °C) with high humidity. A light misting of the cage with lukewarm water may be of additional value in stimulating appetite. Keeping corns' crepuscular (active at dusk) nature in mind, gently introduce the tiniest live pinkie mouse you can obtain into the cage just in front of the entrance to the hide box around sunset. Quickly vacate the room to avoid spooking the shy hatchling. If you feel compelled to return to check progress, wait at least fifteen minutes and do so without turning on bright lights or causing vibrations in the room from your footsteps.

If the first effort fails, repeat the process the following evening, but this time place the snake and pinkie together into an empty deli cup that is four inches (10 cm) in diameter with a few ventilation holes and an opaque lid for privacy. The reason for isolating the snake and pinkie is to give the snake just one thing to concentrate upon all night. The mouse has been gone by morning in about 50 percent of the times we've tried it. To prevent an escape by the snake if the deli cup lid gets pushed off, put the cupped snake inside the snake's cage. Make sure you don't place the cup on top of any heat tape or pad where it could get too hot.

If necessary, the procedure can be tried a third time with a freshly killed pinkie. Occasionally an active pinkie frightens a shy snake too much, so the motionless food item is more enticing. Braining a pre-killed mouse (peeling the skin off the head with tweezers and gouging the brain so bodily fluids are released) exposes a stronger scent that tempts some snakes into action. Some breeders report that leaving the baby corn alone with only a pinkie head works well for them too. Thawed mice have an increased olfactory arousal effect as the skin cells ruptured during freezing exude a particularly strong rodent aroma to snakes. Try the deli cup method at least three times before moving on to more drastic procedures.

When none of this works, it's time to resort to disguise-scenting, replacing the mouse's body odor with the aroma of a different prey species that may trigger an instinctual feeding response. The scent of hamsters, gerbils, deer mice,

Leaving a stubborn baby corn alone with just its intended meal in a deli cup is a method that often results in the snake eating overnight.

other exotic rodents, or their dirty bedding may occasionally work instead of domestic mice (*Mus musculus*) and rats (*Rattus norvegicus*). Smear-scenting a rodent with chicken soup has even worked for one corn snake enthusiast.

Find a treefrog (*Hyla* sp.), anole (*Anolis* sp.), swift (*Sceloporus* sp.), gecko (*Coleonyx* sp., *Eublepharis* sp., *Hemidactylus* sp., or nearly any other gecko species), or other small lizard species that many corns eat in the wild as their first meals. Use it to thoroughly cover the pinkie's odor by rubbing the mouse against the lizard's or frog's moistened skin. As before, body fluids have greater appeal, so breaking the (live) lizard's tail and smearing blood onto the mouse creates a stronger attractant. If one kind of lizard fails to tempt your corn, try others until you find one that pleases the finicky feeder's palate. A partially skinned frozen lizard or treefrog can also do the job and be saved in a resealable plastic bag to be reused many times if necessary.

Some breeders advocate washing baby rodents in warm water prior to any artificial scenting to further eliminate any natural rodent odor that the snake may find distracting. This seems to contradict what we stated earlier, but it has apparently worked for some people.

Tease-feeding

The next tool in your arsenal after scenting is tease-feeding. Fortunately, corns are fairly easy to induce to feed via this method if you can muster the necessary patience. Hold the snake firmly but gently with one hand around its midsection, enclosing its body with a closed four-fingered fist and leaving its tail hanging out below. Only 2–3 inches (5–7.5 cm) of the corn's head and neck should be sticking up free above your curled index finger. With the other hand, hold a small pre-killed pinkie mouse with the head protruding out past your fingertips, and use it to gently tap the snake along the posterior third of its body. A long tweezers or forceps works well for holding the baby mouse because it is less bulky than your fingers and thus doesn't frighten the snake as easily. Avoid touching the snake's head and upper body as this only induces a fright response. The idea is to tease the snake enough to make it strike out in anger or curiosity at the object pestering its flank, but not to send it cringing in fear of its head being attacked. What you hope will happen is that the snake will lunge out, grab the pinkie, and hang on! If it doesn't, try, try again until it finally latches on and decides to keep it.

Now comes the patience part! You must remain dead still—ignore that fly on your nose—and let the baby snake forget about everything except the object in its mouth. It will usually spend from a few seconds to a minute or two "contemplating" the morsel, and then, if you've succeeded in not spooking it, start to swallow. Any distraction at this point may cause it to withdraw and drop the mouse, at which point the next attempt may be even tougher. Remain completely motionless until the lump disappears down the throat and out of sight. Then gently put the snake back in its cage and don't disturb it for a couple of days—you and it need the rest! The good news is that baby corns are usually quick to accept food this way, although the first few feedings may take many attempts before each success, making it a relatively painless process after only two or three sessions. We've found having the TV on while engaged in doing this initially tedious task helps the time pass more quickly.

An idea that sounds silly at first has worked to stimulate appetite in diverse species of herps: bouncing the reluctant feeder around a bit. Speculation exists that a rough ride may stimulate a herp's stomach juices to slosh around and somehow induce hunger in some animals. Reports of sudden feedings have come to us after problem corns were either shipped or transported by car for long trips. We have also noticed that sometimes a change—almost any change—may help. After moving to a new home or even a new room, some stubborn feeders begin to feed spontaneously.

Force-feeding

Force-feeding is the last desperation step in dealing with a nonfeeder, and should only be attempted when the above steps at voluntary feeding fail. Don't resort to this method too soon because otherwise healthy neonates can easily go four weeks without eating, as long as fresh drinking water is present. The routine is potentially dangerous for a fragile little snake and is stressful on snake and owner alike.

Hold the snake as when tease-feeding, but this time leave only its head free. Have a thin, smooth metal or plastic rod, such as the slender end of a knitting needle, handy. If the snake refuses to open its mouth, use the rod to carefully pry it open, trying not to damage any teeth. Insert the nose of the tiniest available pinkie mouse (or a severed pinkie head) as deeply as possible into the snake's throat, keeping a slight pressure on the rear end of the prey so it's not immediately expelled. A little water or butter will help lubricate the prey so it slides down more easily. Use a round-tipped rod to carefully prod it down into the gullet until it disappears from sight, and then gently massage the food down from the outside for at least a couple more inches. Once there, the food will probably either come back out within a matter of minutes or settle down further into the stomach and be digested normally.

Some keepers prefer to use the tails of young mice since their elongated shape makes them easier to force-feed to baby snakes. Tails probably don't provide a lot of nutrition, but they may allow the hatchling to survive long enough for its own feeding drive to kick in.

You can force food into a snake's belly using a plastic hypodermic syringe with a thin flexible tube (such as a human catheter) affixed to the end in place of a needle. For tiny hatchlings, special 3- to 4-inch (7.5–10 cm) stainless steel feeding tubes, obtained from specialty herp dealers or veterinary suppliers, may be attached to 10–20-cc syringes for the same purpose. Fill the syringe with finely ground cat food or strained meat baby food to provide a couple of fast meals to stimulate a snake's appetite. These mixtures may not make completely balanced diets for snakes, though, and should be thought of only as emergency measures. A 1-cc quantity of the formula is enough for one feeding to a baby corn that is 12 inches (30 cm) long. Forcing the mixture through a tea strainer may be necessary if it gets stuck in the feeding tube.

Tease-feeding a stubborn baby corn first involves gently restraining it in one hand while offering a baby mouse to it with the other hand. Ideally, you want the snake to forget the fact that it's being held in your hand and concentrate solely on the pinkie confronting it.

Hold the pinkie inches away from its snout, bumping it against the snake's body or tail—not its head!—until the corn lunges for it. Cease all motion when the snake connects by sinking its teeth into the mouse. At this stage, it's important to entice the snake, but not frighten it.

Don't move a muscle as the snake decides whether to continue swallowing or releasing the morsel in its mouth. Stay extremely still and let the snake finish swallowing the meal before laying the snake back down in its cage.

The Pinkie Pump, and similar devices are custom-made stainless steel syringes that deliver whole dead pinkie mice into baby snakes' stomachs. Pushing the syringe's plunger purées the mice and pushes the resultant broth down a snake's throat via a short hollow tube built into the end, all in one action. Its basic advantage is that it delivers whole food, which is a better diet overall.

An inexpensive electric coffee grinder (acquired strictly for this use) will grind up pinkie rodents (mice or rats) finely enough to go down a stainless steel feeding tube (or slender rubber catheter) attached to a plastic syringe. A tea strainer may have to be used to remove some fragments first so it doesn't get clogged. The coffee grinder works better using several thawed pinkies plus some water. If you make more than is needed immediately, the remainder may be frozen for future use.

When Nothing Else Works

Force-feeding should be performed at the same periodic rate as normal feeding. The technique is not intended to be more than a temporary measure while getting a problem snake "back on its feet." Most baby corns that are kept alive by force-feeding for a couple of months start eating on their own. If snakes can be kept healthy until fall, then put into hibernation with the adults, they may start feeding in the spring with the cues of longer day lengths and warmer temperatures as spurs.

If a baby snake does not start eating voluntarily after a few months of the above measures, it will probably never be a healthy specimen. A very low percentage of hatchlings, despite your best efforts, will persist in their determination to slowly starve to death. At that point, you may have to accept that it just wasn't in the cards for them to survive. Mother Nature intended for them to be food for other wildlife, and nothing you can do will change this. The preferred and most humane method of euthanasia is for a vet to inject Phenobarbital into the heart or body cavity, or by IV. In addition, inhalant anesthetic is considered humane, but also requires veterinary assistance.

The do-it-yourself method of carbon dioxide (provided by dry ice in the same container, but not touching the animal) is the most humane way to achieve a peaceful end to a suffering reptile. Submerging the dry ice in hot water inside the airtight cage will result in the vapor quickly filling the chamber.

Freezing causes painful ice crystal formation, so if this less acceptable method is used, the snake must be rendered unconscious by refrigeration first.

The last method, decapitation, does not immediately stop brain activity. The brain must be destroyed immediately to cause a humane death by any kind of trauma.

CHAPTER 5

BREEDING

Just as fascinating as corn snakes are to keep and enjoy, inducing them to reproduce in captivity takes all that enjoyment to the next level. Successful procreation is the ultimate proof that your care of your snakes' needs has been adequate for them to fulfill the most important function of their lives. It is also interesting, educational, and maybe even profitable to propagate corn snakes as an adjunct to your hobby. This chapter will be handled as one long chronological dialogue to illustrate the subject in detail.

Sexing Corn Snakes

Knowing the sex of corns is an essential first step in efforts to breed them. Sex can be determined with varying degrees of accuracy in many different ways, the most basic of which is simply putting them together and observing which ones actually mate. This will demonstrate the sexes with 100 percent certainty, but it doesn't allow any future planning of pairings. Besides, most corns are acquired as juveniles one or more years ahead of the time they are to be used in reproduction, so judging the sex of them in advance is a necessity.

A successful breeder must personally master one or more methods of sexing snakes to break dependence on others' ability or honesty for that vital information. Mistakes in sexing run rampant in the pet industry and have spoiled many projects when mis-sexed specimens are only discovered after years of raising them to breeding age. Much more often than not, the error turns out to be that a presumed female is actually a male.

Male snakes have an intricate, bilobed sex organ called a hemipenes. Each of the two branches of the hemipenes is

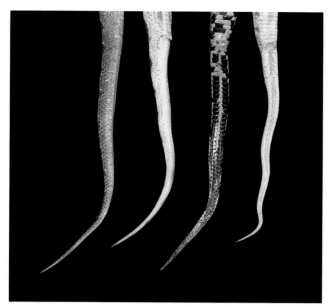

Comparison of tail sizes of males' versus females' tails from side and ventral views. From left to right: male, female, male, female. It's not difficult to judge the sex of adult corns by the relative proportions of their tails. An adult male's tail is thicker (to house the hemipenes) for the first several inches just past the vent, whereas the female's tail base tapers quickly just beyond the cloacal opening. This is especially noticeable once corns are 30 inches (76 cm) or longer in total length.

called a hemipenis. The hemipenes lies in the base of the tail starting just behind the cloaca (the combined copulatory and defecation opening also called the vent or anal opening). The organ's two prongs are rarely exposed except during mating and occasionally briefly during defecation. The hemipenes resembles a pair of red or purplish (when filled with blood) protrusions with small bumps or spines. One or both prongs may be extruded at the same time. If either hemipenis is visible at any other time, something is probably wrong with the animal.

The simplest way to deduce the sex of an adult corn is to visually gauge the shape of its tail, especially the base region. Males have longer tails that run the same width for the first 2–3 inches (5–7.5 cm) past the cloaca toward the tail. Female tails taper abruptly just after the vent, mainly because they don't house the space-consumptive sex organs of the males.

The sexes are not difficult to distinguish after studying and learning to recognize the subtle nuances in tail shape. The skill needed is innate in all of us, related to the ability you have to instantly discern the slightest profile variations of human members of the opposite sex, even from great distances. This method is virtually 100 percent accurate by someone experienced at judging many snakes, but should generally be backed up by probing when any doubt exists.

Popping

Exposing the hemipenes of baby or small juvenile snake with your fingers is fast and easy once you've mastered the knack of it. The method works best on small babies, even fresh hatchlings. It's not as easily or safely done once corns exceed about 18 inches (8 cm) in total length. With the belly of the snakeling facing up, hold the tail between your thumb and index finger, with the tip of your thumb about 1/2–3/4 inches (12.5–18 mm) behind the cloaca. Apply light downward pressure with the thumb tip while also pushing forward toward the vent. If it's a male, this will evert one or both prongs of the hemipenes from the vent as they would when used in mating. They may look like clear, white, pink, or red protuberances about 3/16 to 1/8 inch (5–7 mm) long and as slender as toothpicks. If done gently, the practice is harmless to corn snakes, and the organs will slip back inside and disappear from sight as soon as the pressure is released.

Female snakes have no such extrudable appendages in their tails, although snakes of both sexes have small scent glands that occasionally are visible at the edges of the cloaca. Those glands are never more than 1/16 inch (less than 2

With a little practice, the hemipenes of baby corns can be manually everted by gentle pressure applied by the thumb from the tail forward towards the vent. They usually appear pink or red, but may also look pale whitish or nearly clear. This technique is called "popping."

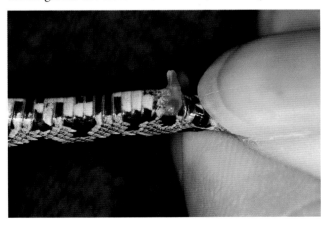

mm), but they tend to fool keepers inexperienced at popping into believing they've seen a hemipenis. Those who have difficulty with this method usually begin applying pressure too close to the cloaca. Start closer to the tail tip of hatchling-size snakes, at least 1/2 inch (12.5 mm) behind the cloaca. If possible, practice with a known male baby before trying to actually determine sex on unknown specimens. It is much easier to perform this task after observing it done in person. Try to find a local reptile shop, herpetological society, breeder, or reptile show where an experienced person is willing to demonstrate the technique.

Candling

Candling is a less dependable sexing method useful on baby corns such as amelanistics that lack black pigment on the belly. It is similar to candling bird eggs for signs of fertility. Use a strong, narrow-beamed light aimed up through a baby amelanistic corn's body from the dorsal side of the tail base region. While viewing this area from the belly side, the hemipenes may be visible as elongated darkened or purplish spots on each side of the centerline of the tail just behind the cloaca. The lack of black skin pigment in amelanistic corns allows the hemipenes to show up through the surrounding clear or white ventral scutes. This organ is not always obvious, but can usually be discerned with some practice involving many specimens for comparison.

Probing

Probing is the standard method employed by most herpetoculturists today to sex snakes of any size or age with high accuracy. This method uses slender metal or plastic rods with rounded tips called sexing probes. Some models have continuous diameter shafts from 4–8 inches (10–20 cm) long; others have wider ball tips to prevent accidentally puncturing the hemipenes when inserted. They are obtainable from many businesses that sell specialty reptile supplies. We have not seen any advantage in the ball-tipped probes when those probe styles lacking ball tips are used carefully and properly. Small corns require small probes which are difficult or impossible to make small enough with ball tips on the ends.

To probe a snake, the round tip of the probe is first moistened with water or a non-oil-based lubricant like K-Y lubricating jelly. Then it is inserted very carefully under the cloacal plate (wide covering scale) at the base of the tail. In males, two tiny openings flanking the cloaca are the entryways to the inverted hemipenes. In females they lead to postanal glands that are very short—1/8 inch (3 mm) deep or less, usually. The hemipenes' basal openings are not readily apparent in most snakes, so gentle exploration with the probe is often necessary to poke around under the vent plate in the direction of the tail. It's best to probe slightly off-center until it slips into one of the two resting hemipenes if they are present.

The probe's diameter should be only 1/32 inch (less than 1 mm) for neonate corns, or up to 1/16 inch (less than 2 mm) for specimens a yard (meter) in length. It is pushed toward the tail with only the lightest pressure so as not to forcibly puncture the organ and penetrate the muscular tissue beyond it. Pushing the probe lightly upon reaching the end of a male organ has a slightly bouncy or springy feel to it; hitting the back of the small pocket of a female's scent gland feels more like a dull thud against something relatively solid. Hemipenes are only about 3/8 inch (9 mm) deep in new hatchlings, but up to about 3 inches (7.5 cm) in large

In a female (top), the sexing probe will barely enter the tail area past the vent. In a male (bottom), it will penetrate to a depth equal to at least four times the width of the tail.

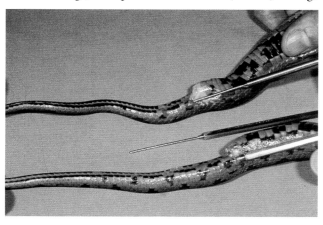

adult males. If the probe enters to that depth on either side without being pushed too hard, you're relatively assured of having a male. A probe will barely enter a female's tail for more than the distance equal to the width of the tail at the vent of any size corn snake. As with the popping technique, practice with already-sexed animals, preferably after being shown how to do it in person.

Pre-breeding Conditioning

Corn snakes follow a fairly typical temperate climate reptilian reproductive cycle, with mating in spring and egg-laying during late spring to early summer. The eggs hatch over the summer, and both young and old go through a variably strict dormant period during the cooler months. Environmental stimuli control the timing of these events annually. Allowing your corns to experience such seasonal changes keeps their internal biological clocks ticking on schedule so these natural events bring about successful breeding in captivity. Even when corns reproduce successfully with no apparent access to seasonal changes, it's likely that tiny changes in environmental cues were noticed by the snakes' bodies. This may have been from exposure to natural light entering a distant basement window, the slight average rise in ambient temperatures following winter, or factors we've yet to completely comprehend.

Many herpetoculturists use manipulation of temperature alone to induce their herps to breed. It often works, and some species apparently reproduce well without a change in photoperiod. In our opinion, temperature and photoperiod are both important triggers of reproduction in corns. Facilitating their impact on successful breeding can be simple to accomplish since each is easy to control in your home. This chapter will help you avoid repeating the fundamental errors of basic herp keeping of the 1950s, when essentially healthy snakes were maintained, but hardly ever reproduced!

The vast majority of keepers maintain their collections indoors, so synchronizing reproduction depends on making their snakes aware of the progression of seasons. This can be done through artificial means anywhere in a home where a cool area can be maintained for two to three months of the year. If the situation also allows natural light to be the main source of daily light for the cages, such as by putting them near an outside window or skylight, so much the better! If the exposure is sufficiently large, the sun may also affect the room (or cage) temperature to reflect the gradually changing trend outdoors. This necessarily links your corns' breeding cycle to your latitude, but it's a tried and true method for positive results.

If your animal-keeping area happens to be in a cool, dark basement in a northern climate, artificial heaters and lights on electric timers can replicate the increasing or decreasing temperatures and day lengths of the seasons. Totally controlling these environmental cues may be expensive but has the advantage of allowing earlier or later breeding and hatching to suit your time schedules or to coincide with better marketing periods.

To better explain replicating a typical reproductive cycle for corn snakes by example, let's assume a starting point for our breeding plans in the autumn, after the main summer active season is over, and follow the typical routine we use in southern Florida. We'll ignore what happened during the previous breeding season and note only that our snakes have been feeding well all summer and early fall, look fat and healthy, and are either already adults or will likely reach adult proportions within months and be ready for breeding the following year. This does not apply to thin or otherwise health-compromised specimens that are best kept separately in warm, well-lit places where they will continue to feed and recover. From all accounts, it is unnecessary to subject juvenile corns to reproductive cycling during their first year of life. You may safely skip this conditioning phase and simply grow them up a little faster with no apparent harm done during their initial warm winter season. Starting them cycling the first year they're of breedable size, typically at two to three years of age (or minimally 30 inches [76 cm] in total length), seems to work fine with no adverse effects noted to their health or reproductive success.

Winter

Look ahead at your schedule for the coming months and choose a date for the start of your snakes' winter dormancy period. We have often designated mid-December as our target date to let the room temperature drop. That, not coincidentally, is just before Christmas and is also (significantly) about the shortest day of the year in the northern hemisphere. At least two weeks prior to that date, or to whatever date you pick, all feeding of your intended breeder animals should come to a complete halt. For those couple of weeks up until mid-December, we maintain the warm temperatures our corns have enjoyed for the last few months to allow enough time for all food to pass through their digestive tracts. We don't want undigested food, or even old fecal matter, resting in the snakes' guts during dormancy to invite contamination or getting stuck from inactivity. Fresh water is kept available at all times, regardless of all other parameters.

When hibernation (also called brumation when applied to herps) begins, windows and skylights are blocked to severely cut the natural outside light intensity. Some people merely draw the blinds or curtains to block off most of the light, which might simulate winter conditions during the cooler months when the sun is less intense and above the horizon for fewer hours. Others advise cutting off all ambient light to superstimulate snakes into thinking it's the dead of winter, as in a subterranean hibernaculum in southern New Jersey.

After the digestive tract flushing-out period, the heat is shut off or at least cut back considerably. The idea here is to let corns experience a cooler period than that in which they're active for the rest of the year. This coincides naturally with the shorter day lengths of winter. Decades of experience have taught us that this period does not have to be very exact or constant, just noticeably lower so the snakes' reproductive systems know it's that time. Spermatogenesis and ovarian follicle development, the internal formation of male and female sex cells, need this cooler rest period. The exact limits of when it starts or ends, or how long it takes, remain debatable. Due to yearly fluctuations in the weather, it's safe to say that no precise formula exists to trigger sex cell formation, nor must one be strictly adhered to in captivity for successful results.

We aim for a cool season in the 45°F–65°F (7°C–18°C) range for about sixty to seventy-five days, but it's not a factor that must be critically monitored or controlled. Corns can handle hibernation periods of three months easily and safely; some herpetoculturists recommend a longer rest, for both the snakes and themselves. Our snake room regularly rises into the upper 70s°F (24°C–27°C), and even into the mid 80s°F (29°C–30°C) during occasional afternoons on the coldest months of January and February with no perceivable ill effects on our colony. When that happens, after all, it's even warmer outside where native corns live and breed in the woods near our home.

Conversely, the thermometer also dips into the upper 30s°F (3°C–4°C) on a few nights most winters, with no detrimental effects from such lows either. We've learned not to fret the odd extremes. As long as they don't persist for more than a few days at a time, and it stays generally cooler for the majority of the dormancy period, that's apparently sufficient to not disrupt a normal winter. Corn snakes' natural range spans 15 degrees of latitude; they are equipped to handle temperature extremes of short duration. We recommend individual experimentation with the intensity of winter your colony is subjected to based on these broad guidelines.

Occasionally, winters bathe southern Florida in unseasonably mild temperatures for stretches of many weeks. One of those ideal tourist winters in the late 1990s was freakishly warm, sparing us from a freeze at all. Severe exceptions like that may adversely affect reproduction because we noticed somewhat lower fertility in eggs the following spring-summer season. We could attribute it to no other reasons, although there may have been some. To combat such phenomena, we've resorted to air-conditioning the corn snake room during excessive heat waves to try to keep it below 65°F (18°C) over those warm spells. A hibernation period consistently above this level can cause snakes to burn fat reserves (when they aren't being fed) and enter the spring reproductive season thinner and weaker than they should be. We barely disturb our corns during the entire two- to two-and-a-half-month cool period. Replacing their drinking water and bowl once per week is the only reason we bother them during that time.

Spring

Toward mid-February, we uncover the windows. A week or so later, we turn on the heat, especially at night, to send a strong message that spring has begun. The salient point we hope to convince the snakes' reproductive systems of is that there's no turning back once the light levels increase and the air begins to warm up. We don't want to allow a late cold snap to disrupt the orderly procession of hormonally-influenced reproductive events in our snakes' bodies, even though nature is seldom so precise.

If you live at a latitude that permits you to maintain your specimens outdoors most or all of the year, or in a room well lit with bright skylights, nature will largely take care of temperature and lighting for you. The lengthening of each consecutive day, combined with the steadily increasing warmth that accompanies it, will be sensed directly by all corns living under seminatural conditions. If your situation calls for depending heavily upon artificial fluorescent lighting to simulate this spring light intensification, it's important to note that most bulbs' output is tiny compared to the sun. Counter by using a lot of bulbs, and place them as close as possible to your animals to enhance their effect.

Many organisms intuitively know the amount of daylight hours per day or the intensity of light that must be surpassed to induce certain biochemical reactions, including those for reproduction. It's part of nature's overall recipe—daily light hours increase in length and intensity as the breeding season progresses. Exposing your corns to the regulated heat and light parameters we've described is beneficial to simulate nature when their housing location wouldn't allow them to know what time of year it is otherwise. Controlling these aspects is not always necessary for corns to breed successfully, but doing so tremendously increases the likelihood of success.

To manipulate photoperiod in a place where there's little or no access to outside light, set the timer for the lights to be on for nine to ten hours when you decide to commence the start of spring. Increase the duration of light by fifteen to thirty minutes every two weeks and continue doing this over the next several months. This reverses the trend of winter, which subjects your snakes to more hours of darkness than light, by increasing the daily photoperiod by six hours over three months' time until the days are longer than the nights again. This is another way of super-stimulating them to know that spring has sprung.

All this effort of simulating spring's arrival to your entire collection at the same time is to assure that corn snake hormones will flow in unison. You want your males' and females' reproductive physiologies to be primed to procreate at the same time. Then, when they finally have access to each other during the period when the females are "in heat," both sexes will be ready and instinctively know how to proceed.

Many keepers with a pair of corns have been surprised by a clutch of eggs without any attempt at cycling their adults. They simply kept a pair of corns together. The snakes' bodies knew when it was time and did what came naturally. We'd guess that some form of unnoticed cycling stimulated them, even if it wasn't obvious. It's important to be aware that this can happen, because occasionally very small, barely adult-sized corns can end up reproducing when the females are not yet ready physically. We recommend separating all corns into individual cages before they reach 2 feet (61 cm) in length to avoid this kind of stress on young females.

Following a few days of warm, digestion-friendly temperatures, a single smaller-than-normal rodent is offered to each of our "awakened" corns. We start snakes on an easily handled meal to assure that their digestive systems are functioning smoothly after the "big sleep." The next meal follows in a week or less and is back to the size and weight that is typical for each individual corn snake. From then on, they're fed to their stomachs' content for several weeks so they put on weight rapidly. This is not to replace ounces or grams lost during winter, as healthy specimens hardly lose any weight. Our real goal is for the females to acquire extra bulk in preparation for producing eggs soon.

Obligingly, females seem to add weight unusually quickly at this time. Many older juveniles also seem to bulk up and suddenly acquire adult proportions during the spring feeding frenzy, presumably in a biologically-governed rush to be available in case the opportunity arises to pass on their genes this season. Ovulation, the production of egg masses in the elongated ovaries, typically starts five to eight weeks after the spring warm-up and posthibernation feeding begins.

Breeding

How do we know when to start breeding our corn snakes in spring? How can we tell when each one is ready? We concentrate almost entirely on our females' physical conditions. Posthibernation shedding, often several weeks and many meals after the warm-up time started, is generally believed to be a reliable signal of the start of the active breeding season. Females may mate successfully then, prior to ovulation, by holding the sperm in waiting until their own egg follicles are mature in a few more weeks. We've noted that matings during this early period typically take longer to be initiated because both males and females seem less eager to breed then, compared to the period after ovulation.

Determining Breeding Time

Experience helps in recognizing the subtle signs of ovulation in females—mainly the bulging posterior halves of their bodies. A moderately stiff swelling may be noticeable in the lower center of their lengths too when it first begins. After we've been feeding females steadily for about a month, we start noticing which ones are bulking up earliest. We begin mentally quantifying the degree of skin showing between their scales and the weight they've gained, especially in their rear halves. Their appearance very much resembles the well-fed look of snakes with recently digested food spread out in their guts, with a couple of slight differences. The bulges tend to be more lateral and soft and squishy to the touch. The belly's ventral scutes take on a more curved appearance, as opposed to the squared-off, flat-bottomed look of nonovulating specimens.

We've perfected a simple little trick to check for ovulating females by feel. Rest the back of your palm on a tabletop, laying a soft, sheer cloth or handkerchief on your upward-facing, slightly spread fingers. Let the female corn in question slowly crawl across your four fingers in a direction perpendicular to them. If she's ovulating, the subtle sensation should remind you vaguely of a string of large pearls bumping along over each finger's hump as it passes. When you get good at it, you can use the same technique to estimate how many eggs there will be or to count the eggs once they are fertilized inside her.

Males have fewer health concerns than females at the beginning of their reproductive lives; it's mostly a matter of whether they will or won't breed, period! We've noticed that young males are often sexually naive during their first encounters with females, crawling around them while not quite knowing exactly what to do next in a discernible show of curious clumsiness. We've seen no harm in trying them early and have noted that they virtually always figure things out within a couple weeks when their next chance to breed occurs.

With young males, or with seasoned larger specimens, don't worry about the males' willingness to cooperate in breeding. Unless they're about to shed (and sometimes even then), when a female is ready to mate, they'll be ready too! Males are sometimes agitated at this time and may occasionally bite stray hands. It's also significant to note that some male corns may only feed sporadically, or not at all, during the breeding season as their sexual appetites seemingly override their need for caloric nourishment. They'll normally resume feeding after the mating season has passed. If not, it helps to remove them from the vicinity of the females. Only on rare occasions have we seen males starve themselves almost to death, and they had to be rescued by a few force-feeding sessions before they decided it was time to resume eating voluntarily. Certain males consistently begin breeding earlier in the season than other males, and some retain interest later into the summer too.

If you don't trust your judgment, you can always revert to the old hit-or-miss method, basing the order of females' readiness to breed solely on the comparative rotundity of their bodies. When we're not certain of which female to try first, we introduce the fattest female that has shed most recently into a male's cage to gauge his reaction. If the female is ready to be bred, she'll be emitting a powerful pheromone—kind of a chemical perfume—that excites males into a vigorous urge to copulate. We feel that it's the male's job to notice this and initiate the action, so we don't want to move him out of the familiar surroundings of his cage as a possible distraction. Other successful breeders use the opposite approach based on the reasoning that it's the males that are less distracted by foreign territory because

Corns mate with their tails raised and joined at the vents. The male (right) everts one hemipenis into the female's slightly gaping cloaca in a split-second pulse after she flags (raises) her tail as an invitation.

they do the most wandering in search of mates in nature. The reality is that it probably doesn't make much difference either way—when they're ready to mate, not much will deter them from their goal.

Misting the enclosure and its occupants with an atomizer bottle of room-temperature water instantly raises the humidity, which enhances the spread and recognition of the female's pheromones. We also, whenever convenient, arrange to introduce snakes on warm, humid evenings when they would naturally be indulging in such activities in the wild. Approaching storm fronts that lower the barometric pressure also seem to stimulate increased breeding excitement in corns.

At this point, all that's necessary is to stand back and observe. The male will usually take an immediate interest in any new snake in his territory. His first task is to determine the snake's sex, usually by crawling forward and examining it with his tongue. He'll often move in a series of spasmodic, jerking pulses when he has any inkling that a female is nearby. He takes particular interest in the cloacal region of the newcomer, where the sex organs presumably are most detectable by scent or pheromones.

If the snake you thought was female is actually male, the resident male may react by violently pushing, bumping, and sometimes biting the other snake along the body. This is not to be confused with the love bites of male-female courtship described below. Two male snakes may thrash about the enclosure in a contest of strength, or one will try to escape frantically. While this may be good exercise, we recommend separating the newly introduced snake and admitting that someone made a mistake sexing it. Try another prospective mate right away while your main male is primed for action.

If the resident male discovers that the introduced snake is really female and the time is right, the male will rub his chin along her length, often accompanying this with an undulating wave motion of his body while lining himself up parallel to her. He'll attempt to line up their tails, sliding his under hers to lift it for easier access to her cloacal opening. Depending on her degree of cooperation, she may lift her tail and gape her cloaca open in a display we call flagging—certainly an obvious invitation to mate when she's at her height of readiness. Males may also occasionally gently bite the heads or necks of females during courtship, although this behavior is much more commonly seen in king snakes. However, male corns never bite females with a violent chewing motion as when attacking a rival male.

When the cloacal openings of the snakes are lined up facing one another, a sudden pulse pushes one hemipenis into the female. It only takes a split second and you may easily miss seeing it until you've seen it happen a few times. Upon careful inspection, a small area of the hemipenis may be visible where the cloacas are joined; it looks light pink or white in color. The tails typically rise slowly upward, partly intertwined and almost side-by-side after five or ten seconds.

The pair stays locked in this position, almost motionless except for an occasional spasmodic twitch by the male. It's important not to bother them during this delicate time since they are more sensitive to distractions by people and may split apart prematurely if bothered. If they are not interrupted, they quietly disengage and go their separate ways after ten to twenty minutes on average. The breakup is sometimes initiated by one snake starting to leave the scene by dragging its still-connected mate for a short distance.

It's important for us to know exactly when, or if, each of our females is physically mated because we conduct numerous breedings designed to cross specific traits. Due to the speed of the whole mating affair, and the fact that we're often working on dozens of pairs simultaneously, it's sometimes difficult to monitor the progress in every cage. The simple matter of using plain paper or newsprint as a temporary cage substrate has two related advantages. It can be inspected for semen after the pair separates from mating since a small, yellowish viscous spillage nearly always follows a successful breeding episode. The evidence of semen is more noticeable on paper than mulch, and a nonpolluted sample can be obtained for microscopic sperm viability analysis if desired.

We've found that allowing males a minimal three-day rest period before being called upon for stud service again seems adequate to give them time to recuperate before further breedings. Although we have adhered to the three-day rest strategy, others feel that only the shorter rest of one day is required to recharge their batteries. It may not be necessary to wait even that long, since males are usually eager to copulate again the next day, if not the next hour. Larger, older males seem to recover and are ready to breed again sooner than younger, less-seasoned ones. Fully mature males may also be capable of more fertile breedings per season. Small first-timer males sometimes seem to deplete their sperm after their first one or two matings, and continued copulations result in a rapidly declining fertility rate in the females they breed.

Some herpetoculturists have suggested that males of some snake species, especially those that experience a cooler and possibly a dormant period, such as corns in the northern portion of their range, only produce a finite amount of fresh sperm for use each season. If this theory is true, then males may use up their resources after a certain number of breedings and only shoot blanks afterward no matter how much rest they get between mates.

Due partly to this uncertainty, we maintain a ratio of approximately one male corn snake for every four to six females, estimating that this is a reasonable number that a healthy, large male corn can service comfortably per season. You may certainly exceed this ratio in a pinch, or you may mate a female with many different males if knowing the genetic heritage of the offspring is unimportant to you. One mating is all that's usually necessary to achieve successful fertilization, but there's no harm in letting a female mate as many times as she wants if you have enough males to spare.

Short-term sperm storage is a documented phenomenon in many snake species. It allows females to develop fertilized eggs during times of hardship when finding a mate may be difficult or impossible in nature. Females can hold viable sperm for weeks, months, and possibly even years until they're ready to ovulate. Only at that (often later) time does actual fertilization occur. This is important to note since it alters the expected gestation period, making the egg deposition date harder to predict. The possibility of sperm storage also must be remembered when acquiring an adult female corn for a breeding project that depends on the next clutch of eggs being fathered by a particular snake in your collection. In theory, a female's clutch of eggs may be fathered by more than one male. The new female's eggs may be fertilized by stored sperm from a previous mate and skew the results of your intended breeding experiment in the coming season and for many seasons in the future if you're assuming the offspring are carrying genes from the males you used.

Infertility

As occurs occasionally in all species of animals, a few males and females are incapable of producing fertile eggs for one reason or another. We have found the problem to be very rare in our collection over the past few decades—well less than one percent. Since we are unaware of any reptilian fertility clinics, we usually try to let the questionable animal physically mate at least twice with two different mates on subsequent years. If no (or very few) fertile eggs are produced, and the mate(s) utilized have successfully reproduced with others of the opposite sex previously, then the animal in question is presumed to be infertile and sold as a nonbreeder pet.

Gestation and Egg-laying

Gravid females usually continue to feed ravenously for an additional three to five weeks after mating before the enlarging eggs in their oviducts make passing food or fecal matter uncomfortable. Their appetites will slacken or quit completely as the females approach their prenatal shed, which is a clue that egg-laying will occur in about ten to fourteen days. However, a small percentage will fast during the entire gestation period or even refuse food before mating. You may still offer food to gravid females, noting that much smaller-than-usual items are more readily

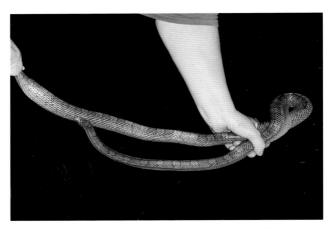

The skin of this gravid female is clearly stretched, and her scales are evenly spread over the obviously heavier rear one-third of her swollen body. She's packed with eggs ready to be laid. Handling should be minimal during this period to reduce stress on the expectant mother.

accepted and are less stressful to digest at this point. Females are often literally bulging by then and have a distinctive pudgy feeling to their rear halves.

Just before the prenatal shed (the one just prior to laying eggs, typically four to six weeks after mating) is the time to prepare a nesting container for the female. Gravid corns seek out a secret, sheltered place with high humidity to deposit a clutch of eggs. If they can't find a suitable spot, they'll drop the eggs in the closest thing available—in a dry hide box or in the water bowl, both of which may spell death for the eggs. Translucent plastic food storage tubs with snap-on lids have proven to be ideally suited for our nest box needs. Not only are they moisture-proof, but they also allow easy visual checking without removing the snake if she's coiled inside. A single round entrance hole about twice the diameter of the female's widest diameter is cut in the top of a box that has the capacity to hold at least two snakes the size of your female. Use a box with plenty of floor area rather than one that's mostly vertical space.

Some kind of moistened material should fill one-half or more of the box to help create an inviting lair. Female corns like to burrow into the substrate and shove it aside to form a nesting cavity, as opposed to laying eggs in a large open space exposed to predators. We've had long-term success using dampened sphagnum moss, although moist vermiculite and crumpled paper towels are fine too.

Translucent or opaque plastic food storage containers with enough interior room to hold two or three adult corns inside make great nesting chambers for gravid corns. Fill each one roughly one-half to two-thirds full of moist sphagnum moss, vermiculite, or damp paper towels, leaving enough room for the female to fit easily inside and comfortably deposit her clutch of eggs.

Vermiculite tends to be very messy, giving the females a metallic sheen as the pieces stick to their snouts and bodies. It may not be the best first choice as a nesting substrate.

As long as whatever you use lacks strong odors or chemical contaminants and holds moisture, it should work adequately. Place the box in the cage when you first notice the female's eyes clouding because she may find it convenient to rest in a moist alcove to hasten loosening her old skin preparatory to the prenatal shed. It will also be a familiar retreat later when she would have to otherwise search for a good place to lay her eggs.

The eggs on the left are healthy fertile eggs, fully filled out and dry-shelled. The smaller ones on the right are infertile judging by their elongated shape, smaller relative diameter and slick, moist appearance.

A clump of normal corn snake eggs typically adheres firmly together in a mass within a couple hours of being laid. The dimples on some eggs are normal and nothing to worry about.

Our corns have generally laid their eggs from thirty-one to forty-five days after mating, averaging about thirty-nine days. This is usually one to two weeks after their prenatal sheds. Many keepers use that timely shed as their cue to place a nest box in the expectant mother's cage and prepare an incubation chamber to later hold the eggs. That strategy will work 99 percent of the time, but corn snakes don't always follow the rules. We've had one bloodline of corn snakes that includes females that routinely lay during the height of their blue-eyed stage prior to shedding.

Corns may be quite active the few days prior to egg deposition if they haven't yet chosen a suitable nesting site. Once they've picked it, though, they seem content to relax and wait, usually inside the container and as out of sight as possible. They may lay the clutch any time of night or day, and the process may span from an hour or two to a couple of days in abnormal cases.

After laying, the mother often remains in the box with the egg mass in a somewhat lethargic state for many days if left alone. As soon as we notice she has laid the clutch, we take the adherent egg mass away. The female rarely offers much resistance to this act aside from some minor shoving with her coils. If she's extremely thin, we offer her one or two fuzzy mice, smaller than her own diameter, right away as a tiny boost before her eyes go opaque again. Some females will accept such snacks immediately; others steadfastly refuse.

Most females have a postnatal shed (one shortly after laying eggs) in about ten days and resume feeding normally soon afterward. Occasionally the strain of carrying eggs wears down a female so much that she has difficulty recovering weight or even holding down meals she normally could handle with ease. We isolate and nurse such specimens with a series of smaller food items, especially thawed fuzzy mice, for ease of digestion until they recover. Fecal exams by a qualified veterinarian may be advised if females refuse food or regurgitate more than once. This may help determine if any pathogens have arisen to take advantage of a female's weakened state and are compounding her problems. Recovering females should be kept away from all other usual cage mates and especially from males that might cause them additional stress in their attempts to breed again.

We've had clutches with as few as four or five eggs from the very first clutch of truly small corns. There was a case in June, 1999, documented with photos by Karen and Joe Street, of a five-year-old amelanistic corn they had raised that laid fifty-three eggs in one clutch. The snake was husky but only about 4½ feet (137 cm) in length. Her eggs were slightly smaller than usual, and all but one or two appeared to be fertile. She has a track record of losing little weight and recovering quickly to double-clutch. This same female, in the 1997 breeding season, first laid forty eggs and later laid a second clutch of thirty-five eggs. All seventy-five eggs hatched and thrived.

Our records show that the average range of eggs per clutch of corn snakes is between ten and thirty eggs. The largest clutch produced from a wild-collected specimen of which we are aware came from a Lee County, Florida, specimen. The snake was acquired gravid by Mark Pellicer. She laid forty-five eggs in one clutch on May 23, 1984, and amazingly, all forty-five eggs hatched out as healthy neonates.

Young or undersized specimens of many colubrid species tend to lay low numbers of physically large eggs. After their second or third year of production, they settle into the routine of laying clutches based more on their individual genetics, with a tendency for the number of eggs in clutches to slowly but steadily increase with the females' increasing age. The quality and quantity of food in their diet for the months preceding breeding may also affect the number of eggs and the size of each egg. Some breeders recommend increasing females' intake of calcium in spring to counter the higher need for depositing shells on their eggs that would otherwise have to come from their own bodies.

Good Eggs and Bad Eggs

Healthy (fertile) eggs are an opaque white or slightly creamy white. Normal egg lengths for individual fertile corn eggs range from about 5/8 inch (16 mm) long and nearly elliptical on the small end of the size range to about 1½ inches (39 mm) in length and quite oblong in shape. They are soft and wet at deposition, with the shells hardening and adhering to those beside them over the next several hours. Upon the residual moisture (from passage through the

This snow corn has just laid a modest-sized clutch of eggs that have spread out in the oversized nest box with vermiculite as the moist substrate medium. Note the tiny, yellower, obviously infertile eggs off to the side.

oviducts) drying, the eggs are generally smooth and tend to absorb a drop of water put on their shells.

Good eggs frequently have, or end up with, numerous irregularities such as rough starburstlike patches, semiclear "windows," stains, discoloration, and oddly rounded shapes on their ends. Most of these are inconsequential and may reflect some imbalance in vitamin and mineral ratios in the mothers' diets. If eggs with such imperfections seem healthy otherwise, there's no reason to try to separate them right away; leaving them in the clump is fine.

Infertile or otherwise compromised eggs are usually smaller, yellowish, and often retain a wet appearance many hours after deposition. They do not stick very well to the other eggs in the clutch, instead tending to roll away and sit alone from the clump. After a few days to a few weeks, they tend to shrink, harden, and become discolored. The changing color and distinct rotting odor will often clue you in, but not all bad eggs follow this exact progressive pattern. We've had some eggs go halfway or more through the incubation period without showing the classic signs just described.

If in doubt, we recommend leaving questionable eggs to incubate normally. Set the suspect eggs off to the side where they're not in contact with the main clump, or put them in a separate container. The vast majority of bad eggs eventually

A bloodred corn is about to pass her last egg of the clutch, which can be seen as the bulge near her cloaca. Except for snapping this photo, we normally refrain from disturbing females during this sensitive time.

succumb to mold or insects, so keeping them away from the good eggs reduces risk of cross-contamination. In our experience, though, that risk is extremely small since healthy eggs are remarkably immune to those problems if correct temperature and moisture levels are maintained.

Corn eggs can be candled to determine fertility in much the same way that is practiced for bird eggs. The simple technique involves focusing a beam of bright, cool light against the shell. Special devices are sold for this purpose, but the same advantageous effect they offer can be easily duplicated by rolling a dark piece of paper around a flashlight and projecting it while the egg is held at the end of the tube. View the egg from the side opposite the light beam or from a 90 degree angle depending upon the intensity of your light source. Look for evidence of blood vessels inside as it glows, which are a sure sign that fertile development is proceeding.

Incubating Eggs

During the late spring and early summer, wild corns deposit their eggs in holes in the ground, in piles of leaves or other organic debris, or in the wood mulch within tree holes.

In captivity, we try to mimic that arrangement by burying the eggs in an incubation medium in a moisture-retentive container. Choose one that has at least enough depth to accommodate a normal clutch—typically about 3 inches (roughly 7.5 cm)—with an additional inch (2.5 cm) or more to spare on all sides as well; you want to leave room for your incubation material to pad the clump of eggs on all sides, including the bottom.

A container that closes completely, such as a plastic shoe box, works well to reduce the drying effect of breezes. Only a few scattered tiny holes—these openings should be less than 1/8 inch (3 mm) in diameter—in the box's walls and lid are needed to let enough oxygen in so that the eggs can breathe. On the other hand, you don't want too much air blowing through so the eggs (and incubation medium) dry out. The main goal is maintaining a high ambient humidity, close to 100 percent, since eggs are mostly water themselves. Their semiporous leathery shells gain or lose moisture as needed, so keeping their surroundings humid allows them to maintain their relative equilibrium easily.

Many materials work adequately as incubation media. Our two personal favorites are sphagnum moss and coarse vermiculite, both obtainable wherever plant nursery supplies are sold. (Read labels and be sure that the vermiculite does not contain fertilizers or pesticides.) Both media allow oxygen to circulate next to the eggs shells while also keeping them moist as water diffuses through the material. We have a slight preference for sphagnum moss since its fluffy composition better accommodates the vertical clumps of eggs that corn snakes usually deposit in our nest boxes. We soak it thoroughly and then squeeze it out as completely as possible by hand to start with the approximately correct level of dampness. The best moisture level for the moss is not precisely measurable—the moss should feel moist, but not be wet enough to be able to wring drops of water out of it.

A 1-inch-deep (2.5 cm) layer of moss is laid down in the incubation container first. The eggs are placed on top, then completely buried in more of the same material so at least

Egg Position

Eggs never have to contend with rotation in the wild; they are left in the same position in which they're deposited for the whole incubation period. This allows embryos to develop the entire time in a stable position within the egg. A small pocket of air forms inside the uppermost area of a developing egg that it is important not to disturb once the embryo starts to grow. The first several days after laying are much less critical, so try to do all moving/adjustments to eggs right away so later rearranging is unnecessary. If any eggs must be moved from their original resting places as they're checked, treated or cleaned, we suggest marking the uppermost surfaces lightly with a pencil (not a marker with wet ink) so they can be replaced with the same side facing up. This precaution is to avoid drowning a developing baby by rotating its head into a lower position within the embryonic fluid or otherwise jarring it from its normal resting position inside the egg.

an inch-thick (2.5 cm) layer pads them on all sides. Pack down a 1-inch-thick layer to act as a lid of moss that can be lifted to expose the eggs underneath when you periodically check their moisture level. This technique envelops the entire clutch in a moist yet airy medium so the shells don't dry and harden, which can make hatching difficult later.

Sphagnum and peat moss contain tannic acid that leaves brown stains on the shells, but its acidic pH is beneficial because it retards bacterial growth. Don't be concerned by the discoloration—it's harmless. It's even possible that bacteria in natural organic incubation substrates contribute a useful function that possibly aids in a slow biochemical breakdown of the shells to weaken them slightly so the hatchlings can escape months later. This benefit has been documented for the hatching of alligator eggs in the nests females construct of plant debris soil, and other materials in Florida.

Combining vermiculite with an equal weight of water achieves a similarly appropriate incubation medium of the right moisture level. The same rule of thumb applies— moist feeling but not wet enough to squeeze water out of it. Large-granule vermiculite with particles approximately 1/8 inch (3 mm) in width is best to allow airflow through it. Its sterile, inorganic makeup also discourages fungi and bacteria unless deteriorating eggs themselves invite attack. Vermiculite works particularly well when the clump of eggs is relatively flat and spread out horizontally or if many eggs are separated and can be buried individually so that only 10–20 percent of each shell is visible. This keeps the threat of desiccation low, yet also leaves a tiny patch of eggshell in view to periodically monitor for problems that might develop.

As when using sphagnum moss, you have to check the clutch once per week to see if the incubation material is getting too dry and add water, if necessary, to the vermiculite around the container edges so it's slowly absorbed throughout the medium. Avoid adding water directly to the clutch where it might drip down onto the eggs and possibly shock them with an abrupt temperature change. Use clean water that's the same temperature as the temperature of the clutch. If there's room, it's handy to keep a small misting bottle of water inside the incubator so you always have some that's a similar temperature.

Rob MacInnes of Glades Herp, Inc., who has successfully incubated thousands of diverse herp eggs over the years, taught us a simple trick that works particularly nicely with vermiculite. Cut a single sheet of newspaper or paper towel to fit the surface area of the egg container and lay it loosely on top of the eggs and medium.

Check the eggs at least every seven days—even more often at first to see if your setup is adequate—by moving the paper to peek at the eggs' condition. At the same time, assess the paper's degree of moistness with your bare fingers. If it's hard and crinkly or the eggs have sunken indentations, add water to the vermiculite around the outer edges of the container away from the eggs. If the paper is wet or slimy and the eggs seem swollen to bursting and feel unusually turgid, it's time to reduce the humidity. Leave the container lid off for a few hours to let evaporation dry it out a little. If the medium seems really damp or moldy, replace some of it with fresh, dry vermiculite.

Amelanistic corns are hatching from eggs incubated in perlite, a soil lightening granulated additive that some breeders prefer. The lowest half-inch of this material may have standing water that evaporates up through it to maintain a high ambient humidity without the actual surface of the eggs coming in contact with wet pieces of the medium. Do not use perlite as cage bedding for hatchlings since it may scratch their delicate skins.

Most people use incubators to assure relatively even temperatures and protect eggs against nighttime drops. The complexities of incubators run the gamut from homemade designs using old aquariums and heating pads (which are not advised!) to technological marvels designed for laboratories or adapted from medical incubators that cost thousands of dollars. Our experience with a simple 18 inch (46 cm) by 8 inch (20 cm) model made primarily of Styrofoam, called the Hova-Bator and made for poultry eggs, has been excellent. Most agricultural feed and supply stores sell them for around fifty dollars, as do some herp dealers. A more expensive model with a small interior fan also is offered but is not necessary for corn snake eggs. Smaller individual egg containers, such as margarine or deli meal tubs or trays (as opposed to shoe boxes) fit within such units and keep clutches separate. Alternatively, the entire floor of the incubator can be covered in sphagnum or vermiculite, and the eggs can be put directly into it without additional holding containers. Babies should be removed immediately upon hatching to avoid possible injuries caused by climbing on and around the incubator's heating element.

With so many other variables between models, our only piece of broadly applicable (and hard-earned) advice is to spend a couple of days setting the unit before any eggs are

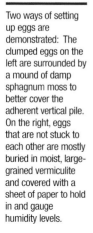

Two ways of setting up eggs are demonstrated: The clumped eggs on the left are surrounded by a mound of damp sphagnum moss to better cover the adherent vertical pile. On the right, eggs that are not stuck to each other are mostly buried in moist, large-grained vermiculite and covered with a sheet of paper to hold in and gauge humidity levels.

trusted to it. Put a quantity of moist incubation medium inside it first to hold heat so the temperature doesn't change dramatically when it's opened for checking. The Styrofoam models described above do not have a simple calibrated adjustment knob, so repeated trial and error microadjustments are necessary at first. A 1- or 2-percent turn of the angled metal knob each time is all that's necessary to make small changes in temperature. Once set, be careful to never bump the knob or to change the setting without careful recalibration and temperature retesting. A hastily guessed resetting of the thermostat may result in an over correction that could possibly result in a fatal mistake.

On any type of incubator, use a good mercury thermometer (the Hova-Bator comes with a hard-to-read but accurate small one) to check temperatures, with the mercury reservoir end buried an inch into the medium that the eggs will soon occupy. That way it's not subject to radical changes when the unit is opened during inspections, letting a puff of cooler air rush in that would otherwise give you a false reading.

Various types of mold, mildew, and bacterial growths occasionally develop on the shells of eggs. White, fuzzy kinds may be an indication of too much humidity or lack of fresh air circulation. Opening the container and allowing it to dry out somewhat retards such growth. Adding a few more ventilation holes to the incubation container will also discourage it. Fluff the incubation medium to let some air get into it, and loosen the eggs themselves if they're stuck in damp pockets within the material. At that point, it won't hurt to also manually rinse the eggs under room-temperature water and pat them dry with paper towels. This wiping technique is especially useful when eggs reach maximum swelling just prior to hatching and develop problems at poorly calcified areas that rupture prematurely.

When green or blue molds appear on eggs within the first two weeks after deposition, it has been, in our experience, a herald of dying eggs. Application of antifungal powders, such as clotrimazole (Lotrimin) recommended for athlete's foot, has been used successfully to salvage eggs under attack. Swabbing the infected areas with a cotton-tipped swab or cloth slightly moistened with Listerine may also work. Do not use sloppy, wet applications that allow excess disinfectant liquids to be absorbed into the eggs through their semipermeable shells, as this may injure the developing embryos.

If the colors return quickly, feel free to try whatever you think may work because those eggs are almost certainly lost. A rotten smell will usually confirm it. At that eleventh hour, it's best to separate bad eggs from any good ones to avoid possible contamination if you don't risk breaking good eggs by doing so. If you do deem separation necessary, carefully cut the infected one(s) away with tiny scissors or a narrow razor blade, being careful not to even nick the good ones in the process. Sop up any residual fluids that come out of the egg being removed. You can leave a small portion of shell of the bad egg attached to the adjacent good egg(s) if it's stuck on tightly—it will not hurt anything.

Cutting away bad eggs is not always necessary. Water sprayed at the junction points will help loosen eggs from the main mass as the offending egg is slowly flexed loose with your fingers, especially in recently laid clutches. Do not use any chemical disinfectants or other potentially noxious fluids that may be absorbed by the good eggs. If the suspicious or bad egg is joined to more than one or two

The dark egg on the end has died and shriveled without affecting the rest of the clutch. Most people remove such eggs with care, though it is not usually necessary.

good eggs, or if it is just difficult to remove, it is not worth the risk to the surrounding good eggs. Just leave it in place to rot after cutting off or sopping up as much of the moist portions as possible. A few left-over attached shell fragments of the removed eggs will not harm the good ones.

Healthy eggs have fully filled-out shells for the majority of their development, only losing their turgidity and collapsing slightly in the last few days before hatching. They actually grow, gaining nearly half their original diameter at laying time over the next two months. Bigger, heavier babies hatch from eggs kept fully hydrated.

If any eggs dent inward or shrink at any time before the eighth week of incubation has passed, they may be suffering from dehydration and need to absorb water. The situation is easily remedied (if the eggs have not sunken in by more than about 40 percent) by wetting the medium adjoining the eggs and thus boosting the general humidity of the box. For a faster fix of severe problems, mist the eggs directly for quick diffusion of water into them, using water the same temperature as the incubator to avoid temperature shock. Cover the eggs immediately afterward to avoid cooling from evaporation. These salvage tactics should be tried on all dehydrated eggs, no matter how hopelessly shriveled they look, in case they can be saved.

It's common for a small percentage of eggs to spoil during incubation, often for no apparent reason. Don't despair—that's why corn snakes lay lots of them! A final hatch rate of 85 to 90 percent is quite good overall in a large collection, although the usual situation in our collection is for most clutches to hatch nearly 100 percent and for a few entire clutches to die and be lost completely. A bad egg virtually never affects the healthy ones attached to it, even if it turns into a kaleidoscope of colored molds or becomes covered in bugs or maggots. We agree with the old assertion that good eggs don't go bad, and thus aren't really prone to attack by something that was only taking advantage of infertile eggs dying anyway.

Elaphe guttata eggs hatch in approximately nine weeks at their optimal hatching temperature of 85°F (29.5°C), but there's a lot of leeway in this very uncritical figure. A range of incubation temperatures, from 70°F–90°F (21°C–32°C), is well tolerated, especially if those extremes only represent fluctuations over the course of the day and not the average for most of it. Maintaining a temperature mostly in the mid 80s°F (28°C–31°C) is what's important for a healthy incubation. Hundreds of clutches of corn eggs have hatched for us over the past couple of decades after an average of seventy-three days of incubation time (the actual range was between sixty-nine and eighty days) following that temperature regimen.

One record was sent to us of a clutch of seventeen eggs that resulted in only one live baby hatching after 120 days, which is abnormally long. This is obviously abnormal and may have involved low, barely tolerable temperatures; genetic defects in the eggs or embryos; or some other problem. Still, it teaches us to never give up on an egg that's taking longer than expected to hatch.

Hazardous temperatures lurk closer to the high end than the low, with exposure to 92°F (33.3°C) for even an hour sometimes proving fatal to eggs. Within the safe zone, we'd narrow the range down to 82°F–88°F (28°C–31°C) for best results. Most people will opt to use an incubator set to maintain an exact reading that doesn't deviate by more than a couple of degrees. Keeping corn snake eggs steadily in this narrower temperature range will hatch corn eggs faster than the average stated above—in approximately fifty-two to fifty-nine days depending on the exact temperature. Cooler or slightly warmer averages can slow or speed up the time by a week or more.

In southern Florida, we usually rely on a very simple method that may be applicable to others in warm climates. It could be dubbed the "summer room temperature method" of placing the containers with incubating eggs on shelves in an insulated room in an outbuilding that's not heated or cooled artificially and that's protected from extremes. In the room, it gets up to about 90°F (32°C) at the end of a hot afternoon, but cools back down to the low 70s°F (21°C–23°C) by morning. The eggs and their incubation medium typically stay a degree or two cooler than the high and a degree or two warmer than the low. We actually feel that moderate temperature fluctuations may be beneficial in a not yet fully comprehended way. Certain functions of embryonic development may progress more naturally in the mildly varying temperatures that eggs usually experience under unstable conditions in nature.

Longitudinal hairline cracks often develop on eggs as they develop and grow. This is normal and does not indicate a problem. Similar "stretch marks" can also appear due to excess moisture absorption by eggs and can lead to malformations or death of embryos. Differentiating between the two is tricky. Judging the moistness of the substrate is a primary clue. If it feels wet instead of just moist, too much moisture may be the problem. Also, if the eggshells feel beyond just being firm—like they're swollen so taut and hard that they seem ready to explode—that is also a sign of the same malady. The remedy is to dry the substrate out the same way as described when initially preparing the nest box.

Late in incubation, eggs virtually always dimple inward, especially during the three to six days prior to hatching. This minor collapse of the shells is normal as yolk is being absorbed into the snakelings' bodies. You may try to inflate them by spraying from the mist bottle at this time if you're unsure, but don't be alarmed if they don't fill back out if you're six weeks or more into the incubation cycle.

Insect Pests During Incubation

Ants, both native and introduced exotics, may discover incubating herp eggs in their extensive wanderings in search of food. They are especially attracted to clutches with problems such as dying eggs. A particularly voracious variety, the Argentine ant, has been a scourge to herp keepers in California as these also occasionally attack snakes in their cages. Accidentally imported Brazilian fire ants sometimes cause the same problems in the southeastern United States.

Specialty ant bait poisons can typically be purchased at garden shops. Bob Applegate recommends a homemade solution mixing a solution of one teaspoon of 1 percent boric acid, three tablespoons of sugar, and two cups of water. Use it by soaking cotton balls in this liquid and placing them inside a small container with entry holes for the ants. They take this weak solution back to the nest, which results in hundreds of dead ants within a few days.

More recent vexations that have begun to plague breeders since the late nineties are infestations of phorid flies. They are tiny flies that quickly zero in on carrion or any other decaying organic substance (feces, shed skins, dead prey items, regurgitations, and hatching eggs) that will offer a meal for them. Entering ventilation holes in egg incubation boxes, especially overly moist ones, they lay huge numbers of their own eggs on or near any dying snake eggs or eggs with punctures. The thousands of eggs hatch within a day or two and result in hordes of tiny, pale maggots looking for food. Another obvious hazard they present is as disease vectors because they forage through snake excretions between cages.

So far, they've been more of an annoyance than threat because healthy snake eggs are not attacked, and the maggots can be washed away once the compromised snake eggs that attracted them are removed. The biggest problem the flies cause is when their maggots get into eggs in the process of hatching and attack neonates before they've fully emerged. They often target the umbilical slit in particular, where they infiltrate and enlarge the opening.

We have responded by covering all ventilation holes on nest boxes with patches of ultrafine mesh—silkscreen mesh works well—applied with a hot glue gun. Care must be taken when closing containers to be certain they are able to seal tightly. Watch for pieces of moss or other material lying over the box edge that leave a crawlspace under the lid that a tiny fly can find to gain entry. If the flies are already present in the room, take care not to let them enter the incubation box when checking the eggs.

Granular fly bait poison (available at feed stores for fly control in animal buildings) can be left out in the room in shallow dishes where your eggs incubate to further reduce their numbers. Be sure to change the bait every few days because it quickly loses the aroma that attracts the flies. Traditional flypaper hung in the room also works well to snag oodles of phorid flies.

Keeping incubation boxes in complete darkness also discourages discovery by flies. Ultraviolet light attracts them, so using bug killers based on that attractant principle works well. We use the ones that drown the bugs in soapy water rather than electrocute them. Moisture provides ideal breeding conditions for flies. The cleaner and drier the surrounding room (and any cages in the room) is kept, the fewer flies will thrive. Keeping the incubation media just moist enough for the eggs, but not overly so, will discourage them as well. Pay special attention to garbage cans, animal cages, sinks and drains, and any other moist or dirty areas.

Hatching

It's been about eight weeks since your corn's eggs went into the incubator, and you are waiting for the great event. Soon, one or more tiny slits start appearing, mostly in the upward-facing portions of the shell of one or more of the eggs. They're formed by a tiny, egg-puncturing projection located at the tip of the snout known as an egg tooth that temporarily graces a hatchling's snout for that purpose. The snake's head then starts to protrude; this stage is called pipping. Hatchlings often pause for minutes or sometimes hours, as this resting period prepares babies for their final

Normal (left) and anerythristic (right) hatchlings emerging from a clutch of eggs. Note the other slits in the shells made by their egg teeth as they worked blindly within their eggs to slice exit openings.

thrust into a new, uncertain world. Some breeders routinely make a starter incision in the shells of any eggs that haven't pipped within twenty-four to forty-eight hours after the first one of a given clutch has started. This helps weak babies escape from particularly tough or thick-shelled eggs.

When they finally emerge completely, baby corns are glossy wet and about 10–12 inches (25–30 cm) long on average. We've known hatchlings as small as 8 inches (20 cm) that hatched normally and survived. Such undersized babies may be perfectly healthy and grow normally, or they may have developmental problems associated with their small size that plagues them forever. As a rule, breeding stock should not be selected from such runts to stem the perpetuation of undesirable traits such as this that may be inheritable.

Specimens emerging from single eggs as twins are usually dwarfed in size but grow at a normal rate. Two sets of twins, one set involving a normal and an anerythristic baby from a single egg (obviously fraternal twins in this case), were hatched in 1998 by Adrian Hemens. The parental stock that produced them shared a recent common ancestor, a hint that the tendency for twinning may be heritable. All four neonates fed voluntarily and thrived. Selectively breeding for the tendency to lay eggs with a high rate of twinning might be a worthy project for a future herpetocultural entrepreneur who doesn't mind getting numerous smaller-than-average baby snakes to feed.

Bicephalism (having two heads) is believed to be an incomplete effort at twinning and has also occurred in corns. Few have survived more than a few months, the exception being a female hatched in 1981 and raised to adulthood by Craig Trumbower. This hardy specimen, dubbed Thelma & Louise at the San Diego Zoo where the snake later ended up, accepted food readily from both heads equally, attained a length of nearly 5 feet (152 cm), and successfully produced eggs before she died.

Housing Neonates

After completely emerging, neonates typically explore their surroundings for several minutes to hours before seeking cover under anything in the container. When we check for hatchlings in clear shoe boxes, we often first lift the box and look up at the bottom from below. If some or all of the eggs have hatched, the neonates are sometimes jumbled together on the bottom in one corner and are easily spotted. Normally an entire clutch will hatch within about thirty-six hours of one another. Unequal heat distribution during incubation may cause a greater range of hatching times, with the warmer eggs being the first to pip.

Shoe boxes or storage boxes make ideal starter cages for baby corns. A variety of models made of plastic (styrene is clear but brittle; translucent polyethylene isn't as easily viewable but resists breakage) are among the most popular choices today. They are cheap, readily available, and the lids either snap down securely or can be held tight with a weight placed upon them. Although not 100 percent airtight, we recommend melting at least a few air holes on all four sides. Each ventilation hole should be less than 1/8 inch (3 mm) in diameter.

The most common shoe boxes are about $6 \times 12 \times 3$ inches high ($16 \times 30 \times 9.5$ cm) and can house a corn comfortably for half a year or longer, depending on growth rate, until it attains a length of approximately 16–20 inches (40.5–51 cm). We prefer clear lids (as opposed to colored lids) that allow quick viewing during maintenance checks without having to remove the lid and disturb the occupant. Medium or large plastic terrariums with brightly colored ventilated tops will work fine and can be purchased for less than ten dollars at most large pet or discount stores.

Substrate materials in shoe boxes can range from a single layer of paper towel or newspaper to shredded aspen. We recommend avoiding aspen for a month or two until the snakes are feeding easily. Sometimes babies have to struggle while learning to subdue their first meals, and they may accidentally ingest pieces of particulate substrate in the process. One-piece substrates such as paper eliminate this hazard and are also easy to check for other signs of trouble, such as abnormal feces, regurgitated food, or uneaten pinkies, during the early stages of acclimation. Removing baby snakes to bare deli cups for feeding is another way of avoiding the ingestion of nonfood material.

For the first few months after hatching, some large-scale breeders have housed their baby corns directly in deli cups 4 inches (10 cm) in diameter. This has the advantage over shoe boxes of saving storage space, and the same cup can later be used for shipping the specimen it formerly housed. Baby mice offered as food are also found readily by snakes in such close quarters, resulting in a higher percentage starting to feed voluntarily this way. On the downside, the deli cup necessitates finding small enough containers to serve as water bowls. Plastic PVC pipe caps are most often used, but with no room for a hiding place the snakes frequently coil in the water, spilling it. Excess moisture buildup can quickly lead to fungus infections in hot, humid climates, particularly when snakes are confined virtually on top of their own feces. Twice-per-week cleaning minimally must be a chore for specimens held this way temporarily.

Baby snakes can safely be sold to experienced keepers moments after they hatch. They are able to survive on their own as long as proper care is taken with them. We, however, strongly recommend a minimal holdback period of two weeks by breeders to get the snakes past their first shed and ideally through the digestion of their first meal. Novice hobbyists should request babies that have fed at least two or three times. Knowing new pets are subject to extensive handling by curious new owners (especially kids), it's wiser to let neonates run food through their systems prior to facing the rigors of being a new pet.

Reabsorption of Eggs

Occasionally female snakes that appear to be swollen and gravid never lay eggs. Assuming you are correct in your prediction of her being gravid, either she reabsorbed the developing eggs into her system or ate the clutch shortly after it was laid. Cannibalization of eggs by mother snakes is extremely rare—we've heard claims with other snake species, but can't document it happening in corn snakes— so the former is probably most often the correct but confusing reality. Snakes can absorb unfertilized eggs (ova) back into their bodies if the time is reached when they apparently will not be fertilized that season. The soon-to-be eggs may have been fully formed and ready to go, giving the female corn the physical appearance and pudgy feel of carrying actual fertilized eggs about to be laid. The lumps may even be countable by feel or visual observation, but never represented eggs capable of furthering the gene pool. If the female in question had mated with a male, the problem in such a case is likely to be that of the male. He may have physically copulated with the female but was impotent and did not actually impregnate her with viable sperm.

If a female corn snake ovulates after mating (regardless of whether it was a fertile mating), which probably happens in captivity more often than in the wild, the bulging of her belly from ovulation may occur about the time you expected her to start looking gravid. This has fooled many keepers into thinking a clutch of eggs is imminent, only to be disappointed as the weeks pass and the female slowly regains her normal appearance. However, if the eggs were never, in fact, fertilized at all, they may just be reabsorbed into her body with no trace left behind. The phenomenon of ovulation coming after mating must take place because we've seen numerous female corns lay their eggs up to a month after others that have bred at the same time and that were kept under identical environmental conditions.

Double-Clutching

As references in the preceding discussion indicate, corn snakes are quite capable of laying more than one clutch of eggs per season. Although this is certainly a very rare event under purely natural conditions in the wild, it occurs with moderate frequency in captivity where conditions for reproduction can be closer to ideal. Special husbandry practices will increase the likelihood of obtaining healthy second clutches of eggs from some corn snakes. Not all corns may be genetically disposed to be so prolific, so following these instructions may not guarantee success.

Proper conditioning for hopeful double-clutching begins before the first breeding of the season. Heavy feedings two or even three times per week upon emergence from winter cooling allow a female to enter reproduction with abundant body reserves to produce a first clutch of eggs with minimal stress to her body. Her diet should consist of quality food items that have in turn been fed balanced diets.

Ideally, a female corn snake should not have to reduce her bulk substantially to produce eggs, but in the unpredictability of nature that isn't always possible. Some females literally forsake everything, including their own health, toward procreation. Often they are depleted physically as their bodies are drained of muscle mass, calcium (bone strength), and trace minerals in an effort to send their eggs forth with sufficient nutrients to assure the embryos' survival. If a female appears considerably thinner and more bedraggled after laying her first clutch of eggs, she is probably not a candidate for attempted double-clutching. To the contrary, if the female is not much skinnier than before laying (if she seems to have lost less than one-quarter of her prenatal bulk) and has no trace of a protruding backbone ridge, she may be able to handle the strain of producing a second clutch of eggs in one season.

It is debatable whether a corn snake that can lay a second clutch will proceed in automatically developing those eggs within her body. Some breeders feel the "decision" is based purely on a female's bodily resources having the ability to physically supply the materials. Others suspect hormones from other corn snakes nearby during the height of mating season may influence females to ovulate again if their bodies receive the other corresponding cues of continuing heat and photoperiod. The fact remains that many corns that can lay a second clutch will, so it's best to be cognizant of that fact and watch for it after all first clutches are laid. An indication that a second clutch is on the way may be that a female stops feeding after only a few postnatal meals. If she has not seen a male after laying the first clutch, a smaller clutch may be arriving. The cycling time in our colony between first and second clutches results in the female laying her second clutch very close to the time her first clutch is hatching.

Large-scale Reproductive Data

The following reproductive data were tabulated for the largest known colony of corn snakes in captivity, which was managed intensively for maximum offspring production over the seven-year period spanning 1997 to 2003. The data clearly illustrate the potential productivity of *E. guttata* on a statistical level based on thousands of breedings. Accurate large-scale data has never before been available for analysis. We feel privileged to be able to include this information, tallied from Bill Brant, Joe Hiduke, and Adam Black's detailed records at the Gourmet Rodent, Inc., Archer (Gainesville), Florida.

Intensively farmed female corns laid an average of nearly 17 eggs per clutch on their first clutches; 14.2 of them on average proved to be fertile—slightly more than 84 percent fertility. When second clutches were factored in, the average overall number of eggs per female increased to 26.4, but the overall fertility rate dropped to 74 percent for the year.

Reproductive Chart

Seven Year Large-scale Corn Snake Farming Reproductive Statistics

	1997	1998	1999	2000	2001	2002	2003
Total # of females in the collection deemed to be potentially breedable (mature) in the spring of the given year.	250	262	504	730	828	1087	1720
Total # of 1st CLUTCHES OF EGGS	232	260	489	693	761	1074	1653
Percentage of females laying 1st clutches	92.80%	99.20%	97.00%	94.93%	91.91%	98.80%	96.10%
Total 1st clutch egg production (fertile + infertile)	3866	5056	8563	11350	12729	19298	30360
Total 1st clutch eggs (fertile only)	3205	4460	7683	9868	10664	15163	24311
Percentage of 1st clutch fertility	82.90%	88.21%	89.72%	86.94%	83.78%	78.57%	80.08%
Average # eggs per female	15.46	19.3	16.99	15.55	15.37	17.75	17.65
Average # fertile eggs per female	12.82	17.02	15.24	13.52	12.88	13.95	14.13
Total # of 2nd CLUTCHES OF EGGS	211	207	408	540	590	737	1210
Percentage of females laying 2nd clutches	84.40%	79.01%	83.44%	77.92%	77.53%	68.62%	73.20%
Total 2nd clutch egg production (fertile + infertile)	2545	2447	4850	5503	6603	9131	14967
Total 2nd clutch eggs (fertile only)	1652	1041	3130	3553	3882	5868	9071
Percentage of 2nd clutch fertility	64.91%	42.54%	64.54%	64.56%	58.79%	64.26%	60.61%
Average # eggs per female	10.18	9.34	9.62	7.54	7.97	8.40	8.7
Average # fertile eggs per female	6.61	3.97	6.21	4.87	4.69	5.40	5.27
Elaphe guttata – female reproductive stats for a seven year period in captivity							
Average # eggs per female (1st and 2nd clutches)	25.81	28.64	26.61	23.09	23.35	26.15	26.35
Avg. # fertile eggs per female (1st and 2nd clutches)	19.45	21.00	21.45	18.38	17.57	19.35	19.41
Average # of clutches per female	1.78	1.78	1.78	1.69	1.63	1.67	1.66

Females averaged laying 1.7 clutches each per season. The average number of fertile eggs in second clutches dropped to 5.3 on average, a fertility loss of 63 percent from that of first clutches. Producing a second clutch of eggs is hard on females. Clearly this is reflected in much poorer production results too, but from a farmer's perspective the extra 5.3 eggs per female come at relatively little extra time or expense annually. An individual pet keeper lavishing extra food and attention upon a small collection he or she maintains intimately might be expected to increase these numbers.

CHAPTER 6

DISEASES AND DISORDERS

B esides the problems discussed earlier under shedding and breeding, corns are subject to the same array of disorders that can affect many other kinds of snakes. In their defense, we must emphasize that E. guttata is among the hardiest of all snakes kept as pets today. Captive-raised specimens especially have a rather low probability of suffering from any of the maladies discussed in this chapter. We've chosen to discuss them in descending order of likelihood (except for the final one) based on our years of dealing with tens of thousands of individuals. This chapter is more like a first aid course. We urge you to seek the aid of a qualified veterinarian for serious problems that do not respond to the basic treatments we've outlined. The veterinary reference books listed in back are also excellent and very current in their more in-depth discussions of these subjects. You can also access a list of experienced herp vets, categorized by their resident state or country, at: http://www.herpvetconnection.com.

Isolate a specimen with any kind of problem to avoid passing the malady (such as parasites or diseases.) on to healthy animals and to reduce stress on the inflicted individual. Give the sick snake the option of choosing its own preferred temperature by offering a gradient across the cage's length with either an undertank heat tape, or a heat lamp aimed at one end of the enclosure. Provide plenty of hiding places—a hollow log as long as the cage works well—so the snake can remain hidden while choosing the best distance from the heat to attain the ideal recovery temperature. Set the patient up in a quiet spot, and curtail all handling and unnecessary disturbances as you determine the exact nature of its problem and decide upon a course of special treatment.

External Parasites

Mites

Mites are pinhead-sized (1 mm) arachnids most often noticed bulging like tiny balloons from the skin of snakes. They also appear as tiny black or red beads crawling around over snakes' bodies. Mites feed upon blood, which they extract by their sucking mouthparts while imbedded between scales. Red mites infest wild snakes mostly and have never plagued captive collections after being initially removed. The black ones (the common snake mite *Ophionyssus natricis*) are slightly larger and have evolved to parasitize herps as adults. These mites multiply rapidly and can cause lethargy, dehydration, or anemia in their victims when present in large numbers. Their travels throughout a collection can also make them important vectors of disease.

If unsure of a mite infestation, first check the water bowl for dead ones that fall in and drown. Their bodies look like grains of coarse pepper on the bottom of the bowl. Another simple test is to let the snake in question crawl through your snugly clenched fist so that it rubs its entire length against your fingers. This will almost surely dislodge some mites onto your skin, where they're easily seen as they move about. Also look for them around snakes' eyes, in the mental groove (chin), and between all the large head scales. Snake mites don't bite people, so they're not a personal concern to handlers. Do the examination over a sink so you can wash your hands and fingernails on the spot and rinse snakes to start the removal process immediately, if necessary. Severe infestations of black snake mites may actually give the snake itself a peppered appearance or a salted one if the whitish feces have accumulated in sufficient quantities.

An old and simple method of treatment is to place the infested snake in a plastic jar or box filled with water to a depth that's higher than the snake's girth. The lid should be perforated to allow for air flow and weighted down or taped shut. Leaving the snake to soak for ten minutes will drown most mites; an hour is all it should ever take. Monitor your snake during this process to be sure it doesn't encounter undue stress trying to escape or get stuck in an awkward position that might cause it to drown. A few drops of liquid soap added to the soaking water reduces the water tension, which cuts down on air pockets under and around the snake's scales and drowns mites more quickly. The only drawback is that some will migrate up to the head and survive. These can be manually removed under a rushing spigot or by gentle rubbing with a damp cloth. A dab of petroleum jelly or a drop of mineral oil over a snake's eye will suffocate mites buried around the ocular scale. Older references describe coating the entire snake in vegetable oil for an hour to suffocate mites. This will work, but yuck, what a slimy mess to clean up! Please note that none of the above drowning treatments may kill all of the mites the first time. These methods usually require reapplications to be fully effective.

An ivermectin spray consisting of 5–10 milligrams (mg) of liquid ivermectin to a quart or liter of water can be applied directly to snakes and their cages (minus the water bowl) to destroy mites. It's best to repeat the spraying weekly for several weeks to get all stragglers.

We have used a "shake and bake" method in which a snake is dusted inside a bag of dry 5 to 10 percent Sevin dust. This product is sold in plant nurseries to control plant pests, but it's not officially sanctioned for use on snakes. In our experience, Sevin dust appears to be harmless to snakes if not ingested or left clogging their mouths, nostrils, or vent. We thoroughly wash specimens off after the treatment, and then we take the additional precautionary step of scattering some Sevin dust on the shelves and floor to prevent odd mites from migrating around the area.

Pest Strips impregnated with the insecticide Vapona (dichlorvos; 2,2 dichlorovinyl dimethyl) are an old and effective method of mite eradication. Small pieces of the strips are left in or near cages so their chemical vapors are emitted. Air movement is limited to allow the vapors to build to a toxic level. The big problem is to judge the dosage of such a treatment since the chemical has also proven toxic to snakes, especially young ones. We no longer recommend Vapona to kill mites due to the fact that a fail-safe regimen of usage cannot be adequately described.

A plethora of new products has emerged in recent years, with varying reports of success. Keeping and breeding captive-bred corns does not really provide us with much need to test new mite products. Since Sevin dust has worked perfectly for us in the past with no unwanted side effects, it is doubtful that we would have any reason to try new products when such an effective, accessible, and inexpensive solution already exists, even if not yet sanctioned for this use by a government agency.

CAUTION: Treating snakes that are in the shedding process is not recommended. There may be a greater risk for pesticide absorption as well as unnecessary damage to the skin when handling. Also, do not combine multiple chemical treatments at the same time, as their effects may be additive and potentially toxic to the snake.

Mites are easy to kill on snakes' bodies but more difficult to eradicate from a collection or room. Regardless of the extermination methods used on the snake, resign yourself to soaking all cages and cage furniture, dipping them in a strong (10 percent or greater) liquid chlorine bleach and water solution for at least ten minutes. If all particulate matter is brushed out first, this should let the bleach reach all parts of the cage and kill all eggs and hidden mites.

Ticks

Ticks are usually brown to gray and from 1/16–3/16 inch (2–4.6 mm) in length when they first appear, attached by their mouthparts, to an area between or partially under the snake's scales. They stay in place and slowly expand as they suck blood, occasionally reaching 1/2 inch (12.5 mm) or more in diameter when fully engorged. They're mostly a concern on wild-caught snakes and aren't predisposed to making an ongoing nuisance of themselves in captivity. When outbreaks occur on a caged snake, they can usually be attributed to the sudden growth of a group of tiny immature ticks that went undetected earlier on a recently collected specimen. The same methods that rid snakes of mites will kill ticks too, although they often remain embedded in the skin when they die. Simply picking them off with tweezers works well whether they're live or dead. Be sure to grasp the tick by the head, not by the body. Squeezing the belly may expel ingested blood back into the snake. A dab of irritating fluid such as alcohol or ammonia often persuades a tick to loosen its grip for easier removal. A small gob of petroleum jelly over a tick also works by cutting its oxygen supply and slowly forcing it to release to breathe. Try to get the imbedded mouthparts out too so they are not left in the skin to possibly cause infection.

Ants

Ants occasionally invade snake rooms and cages in search of food. Food for ants may include uneaten rodents, feces, shed skins, or even living snakes or their eggs. The introduction of several new tropical species, notably Argentine ants and white-footed ants in the warmer climates, has increased the threat because they breed quickly without their natural enemies. They may also have more aggressive foraging habits than our native types, which makes them greater disease vectors.

In recent years, various insect growth regulators have been used to safely control ants and other pests. Consult a professional pest control company to ask about the use of these products for your particular problem.

We've recently been using diatomaceous earth to control ants and other insects in and around our herp buildings. Spreading it around as a light dusting where these little pests regularly roam in the room is like making them walk over broken glass barefoot. Specifically, it kills insects by cutting into their waxy cuticles and causing them to die from dehydration. It's harmless if it gets on or is ingested by you or your snakes, so it's safe to use even inside snake cages.

However, avoid breathing the fine powder by using a mask when applying it. Be sure to use food-grade diatomaceous earth, supplied by feed stores or health food shops, rather than the swimming pool filter-grade. We expect that it would also work effectively on mites if the "shake and bake" method discussed for Sevin were used.

Digestive Disorders

These encompass an assortment of symptoms including poor appetite; chronic weight loss; wasting away; diarrhea; and stools abnormal in coloration, consistency, or smell. Regurgitation of complete or partially digested food items may also be indicative of something more sinister than simple nervousness from lack of a secure hiding place to digest meals or from maintaining animals under too low or high temperatures. Bacterial, protozoal, or viral infections, which require microscopic identification or other diagnostic methods, may require a sample taken from the digestive system of the suspect animal. For proper investigation and identification, growing a culture from the sample in a lab setting may be necessary. Treatments must often be precise in their dosages and timings, and we recommend consulting a qualified reptile veterinarian.

Before assuming the worst, you may want to try the kind and gentle, noninvasive approach of nursing a sick corn snake back to health. Eliminate as much stress from its life as possible, even if it means not seeing or handling your pet as often as you like. Make sure a temperature gradient exists across the cage that's conducive to proper digestion with a range of 75°F–88°F (24°C–31°C). Keep fresh (never more than three days old) drinking water available for whenever the debilitated corn wishes to drink.

It is very important to make sure that digestive/regurgitation problems are cured quickly. Each repeated occurrence weakens the snake and makes it more likely that it will never recover, so treat this issue seriously! The smaller the snake, the faster the problem threatens it.

We have developed a protocol over the years for dealing with regurgitation in corns. If your snake partially or wholly regurgitates any meal, rest the snake for at least eight to ten days. Conduct no feeding, handling, or other activities that may increase stress during that time, and keep it in a cage separate from any other reptiles. The next feeding should consist of an item of no more than 50 percent of the mass of the regurgitated item; smaller is even better. If the snake is a baby, then just the head of a pinkie mouse may be sufficient. Using a previously frozen pinkie is helpful because freezing breaks down the cellular walls to allow faster digestion of the mouse's entire body. If digested successfully, feed the same size item again in five or six days. Then advance the prey size very slowly—take at least a month or even two to work back up to the size that resulted in the regurgitation. If regurgitation occurs again due to moving too quickly to a larger item, then go back to the very first size and start all over. If the snake can't hold down anything at all, it probably has a more serious problem and will need to be seen by a qualified reptile vet.

A mouse of any particular size may be digested more quickly and easily if its skin is sliced or punctured or it is cut in half lengthwise. (Cutting in half can also be a cost-saving measure, allowing you to make two meals out of one pinkie or fuzzy that is too large for your snake. Slice it when the pinkie is still mostly frozen for easier, less messy halving.) Digestion can also be aided by crushing the internal structures of the pinkie before making any cuts into the skin. Preliminary experimentation by Connie Hurley DVM has shown that growth rates of healthy neonate corn snakes increased significantly when they were fed a diet of pinkies that were perforated by at least one deep cut into the body cavity prior to ingestion.

Bacterial Overgrowth in the Intestinal Tract

A vet may treat microbial digestive problems with metronidazole (Flagyl) or sulfadimethoxine (Albon), or you may wish to first try the natural remedies listed below. Some snakes with generalized ADR (Ain't Doin' Right), nasty-looking stools, or chronic regurgitation may simply have gotten their normal gut flora out of whack and have had the bad bacteria and other microbes overgrow and get out of proportion with the good microflora. An infection may not be the problem as much as an inappropriate flourishing of some microbes, which leads to excessive bacterial endotoxin production and illness, diarrhea, regurgitation, and ultimately failure to thrive. This is one of the reasons that resting (giving no food) snakes for a week or two sometimes helps. Remove the excess of nutrition to the bacteria and let them die back to more normal numbers. A short course with one of the above drugs may also help swing the tide, along with warmer temperatures and good hydration.

We've been trying some alternative remedies in recent years. Grapefruit seed extract has been a known suppressor of bacteria and fungi in agriculture for decades and is available for human use at health food stores. A few drops added to the water bowl, after a three-day period of withholding water to ensure thirst, have yielded encouraging results with young corns prone to regurgitation. Be careful, though, because too much extract in the water will result in the snake refusing to drink it. Mix it in a glass and taste it first if in doubt. We have used it on ourselves with some success over the past few years, so don't worry about ingesting it. It is possible that this remedy could change the body chemistry of the snake to some degree. If you seek veterinary treatment, be sure to mention using the grapefruit seed extract in case the medicine dosage being tried needs adjustment.

NutriBAC df is a probiotic product that combines seven different species of beneficial intestinal microflora to replace those that have been lost due to medication, stress, or disease. We have had some early success treating digestive disorders by either rolling small food items in the powder or, in advanced cases where no meal is being held down, using a tube to administer a mixture of water and NutriBAC df. So far we feel it has saved the lives of at least two chronically regurgitating snakes. We have seen no adverse effects and feel it is worth experimenting with. We promote continuous experimentation with new remedies to see if they lead to useful cures.

Internal Parasites

Parasites include a wide variety of organisms that cause many of the signs (weight loss, weakness, lethargy, dullness of skin) mentioned above. They range from one-celled amoebas and coccidia to tapeworms that can be many times longer than their hosts as they wind through the host's intestine. Protozoa often invade the gut wall and cling to the walls of the digestive tract, where they irritate the lining and lessen the host's ability to absorb nutrients. The larger types of parasites, such as roundworms and flukes, are mostly a problem of wild-caught specimens that retain parasite loads for long periods after capture. The use of praziquantel (Droncit), fenbendazole (Panacur), or metronidazole may be warranted. Consult a qualified reptile veterinarian for proper diagnoses and the correct drugs and dosages.

The key to dealing with other gastrointestinal parasites successfully is to first identify the culprit(s). Clues may be found by examining a fresh fecal sample under a microscope to look for the minute organisms, eggs, or even whole worms or pieces of them. Certain larger kinds of parasitic worms such as flukes may even be visible clinging inside a snake's mouth as it yawns, or segments of tapeworms may peek out of the cloaca as the snake defecates. Once you identify the parasite type, you can probably use a specific vermifuge for that family of parasites to purge it, even if the treatment is primarily intended for use in large animals of agricultural importance. Some deworming medicines can be purchased by anyone at feed and farm supply stores; others will require a prescription by a veterinarian.

To administer vermifuges correctly, the stricken snake must be accurately weighed since the amount of cure is often critically linked in a ratio of mg of medicine per kilograms (kg) of the patient's body mass, and overdosing can lead to toxicity to the snake. The following drugs and dosages are the ones most currently recommended by the top vets in the United States for the listed parasites. These drug dosages may change as new knowledge accrues, and new drugs will constantly become available, so we cannot overemphasize the wisdom of consulting an experienced herp veterinarian for professional help in curing snakes with severe cases of these potentially deadly and contagious organisms.

- Amoebas and other protozoans: Metronidazole is the drug of choice for treating these parasites at 25–50 mg/kg of snake, given orally. Recent advice from leading herp vets suggests a widely varying dosage protocol, depending upon circumstances. Consult an experienced herp vet to base individual treatments on a case-by-case basis; it is not possible to generalize. Toxicity is seen at larger and longer dosage schedules, manifesting itself as neurological abnormalities, tremors, and loss of coordination, although these effects may disappear when the drug treatment is withdrawn. It's urgent to clean the snake's cage thoroughly after every defecation during this treatment to prevent recurrence.

- Coccidia: Sulfadimethoxine at 90 mg/kg for the first treatment, then 45 mg/kg over the next five to seven days. A fecal check should be done then to check the treatment's effectiveness. Cryptosporidium is a coccidial parasite that is untreatable by present methods. It is the most dreaded scourge of corn snake collections. It's an invasive protozoan that inhabits the intestinal tract, causing regurgitation and weight loss in infected specimens. A thickening of the stomach, which appears as a mid body swelling in snakes, is a telltale sign in well-advanced stages. Transmission to new hosts is by oral intake of infected liquids, food, or feces. Cryptosporidial disease (crypto) may kill snakes slowly, in up to two years, thus putting every other animal in a collection at risk of infection. This disease is presently incurable, so specimens harboring it should be completely isolated from all other healthy herps at the very least. Because of crypto's extremely infectious nature, experienced collectors recommend destroying infected animals immediately. Veterinarians can perform a screening test involving acid-fast stains during fecal examinations to detect its presence in new specimens before they enter an established herp colony.

Several negative fecal results may be necessary to ensure a snake is free of crypto.

- Nematodes/roundworms: Use fenbendazole at 50–100 mg/kg once per week. This is a rather innocuous drug that has a wide margin of safety. It is effective against spiny-headed worms, hookworms, roundworms, pinworms, and most tapeworms. It's a good broad-spectrum anthelmintic. It doesn't hurt to dose weekly, but most vets dose every two weeks until a stool sample comes up negative or the drug is administered for four consecutive dosages. Another safe anthelmintic drug is pyrantel pamoate (Nemex, Strongid) at 25 mg/kg daily for two to four days, then repeat in three weeks. It does not kill tapeworms, though. Ivermectin (Ivomec, 1 percent injectable) at 0.2 mg/kg (200 micrograms/kg) can be given orally or by injection, repeated in two weeks. While this works well for snakes, never use it on turtles because it has fatal consequences.

- Tapeworms and flukes: Use praziquantel at 5 to 10 mg/kg orally or injected, repeated once after two weeks. A fecal exam two weeks after the last treatment in any of the above parasite cases can be helpful to ensure eradication. Many of the dosage regimens used for reptiles are extrapolated from dog and cat research and are only good estimates.

Salmonellosis

Certain strains of salmonella bacteria have been found to be normal gastrointestinal inhabitants in many reptiles and often will not cause disease symptoms in healthy specimens. However, other pathogenic (illness-producing) strains can cause digestive disorders. In captivity, a combination of nontypical or infected foods and the host's inability to self-regulate its environmental conditions such as inadequate temperatures, as well as stress, can allow salmonella to build up to excessive levels in the gut. It has long been known to be present in foods for humans such as raw chicken and eggs, but it can also be transmitted by most other animals.

Signs include bloody diarrhea, weight loss, inactivity, and dehydration. Should an animal show signs of disease associated with salmonellosis, a qualified reptile veterinarian should be consulted for treatment.

Salmonella can be difficult to eradicate in reptiles for several reasons. It is often only shed in the feces intermittently, which can make diagnosis difficult. It can also go dormant within the body and thus be undetectable for long periods. Additionally, salmonella has the ability to quickly develop resistance to conventional drugs. You can prevent transmission to humans by thoroughly washing any part of your body that was in contact with a suspected carrier, its infected cage, feces, or any bodily fluids. This should be a standard practice after handling any herp! A solution of liquid chlorine bleach in water, in a ratio of 1 part bleach to 9 parts water, kills the salmonella bacteria within ten minutes of constant exposure, as do many other disinfectants such as Roccal-D and chlorhexidine diacetate (Nolvasan). Avoid using cleaners containing phenols such as Lysol and Pine-Sol, which are toxic to corn snakes.

Most human health organizations recommend avoiding contact between reptiles and very small children (who tend to put everything into their mouths) and any other people who have compromised immune systems. It pays to be attentive to the potential threat of salmonella since it has been documented to have been contracted from reptiles, but also know that this pathogen is more commonly transmitted to people by undercooked poultry and eggs from the supermarket than from reptiles. We do not personally know, or know of, anyone who has ever contracted salmonella from reptiles.

Skin Ailments

Corn snakes heal remarkably rapidly from injuries to their integuments (skin). Any surface damage usually accelerates the frequency of shedding to aid in regeneration of skin and scales.

The most common types of dermal injuries come from burns from unshielded or malfunctioning heating devices.

The best way to avoid this is to imagine whether it would be physically possible for your corn snake to press itself against or wrap itself around whatever supplemental heating device you're using. If there's a way, they'll figure it out sooner or later and cram themselves into a position that burns them before they can escape. You'd think it impossible that they could act so stupidly, until the day you're faced with treating the "open wound that couldn't happen." Treatment is much more difficult than prevention, so heed this warning. For minor burns, daily application of a topical antibiotic such as antibiotic ointment (neomycin, bacitracin, polymyxin B, and Polysporin) or silver sulfadiazine cream (Silvadene Cream) daily to the affected areas should be performed until healing occurs. Place the snake in a clean, sterile enclosure free from abrasive or rough substrate and cage furniture. Be sure to keep the water clean and fresh, and avoid particulate substrates that will stick to the wounds or ointment. For more severe burns, consult a qualified reptile veterinarian.

Another common skin injury occurs from snakes getting stuck on tape. Whenever tape such as duct or masking tape is used for any reason in a snake's vicinity, the snake seems to manage to lift up an end and get stuck on it, often tearing its skin in the process. Vegetable oil will help loosen tape glue and get it unstuck, but it may take several sheds to repair the skin damage. The best treatment is prevention. Never use tape within the snake's enclosure.

Bites

Bites from live prey are also familiar to most keepers. Avoiding bites should be intuitive, but there will be times when a live rodent is left in a cage unsupervised over an extended period "for a good reason." It's an excuse we hear often, so you may confront it someday. Clean such wounds with a sterile saline flush or alternatively use a clean water flush, and then apply Betadine solution, diluted with water to the color of weak iced tea. It has a good residual effect after application and works by releasing elemental iodine.

Hydrogen peroxide can be used to cleanse most superficial skin wounds, but not for deep wounds, because it oxidizes and destroys tissue that it comes in contact with. A good substitute cleanser, but not as easily accessible except from a vet, is chlorhexidene diacetate diluted until it is barely blue-tinged. Afterward (for open wounds only) apply an antibiotic cream such as Neosporin, silver sulfadiazine cream, or one of the nitrofurazone (Furacin) creams meant to speed healing in people. Avoid such creams for puncture wounds because they won't get down into the wound and they will block the exit for draining if needed. For punctures, just clean the wounds with Betadine or chlorhexidine diacetate, but don't use any kind of ointment.

For injuries covering areas larger than 1 square inch, a sterile patch can be taped over the area to prevent infection and further abrasion. Place the injured snake in its cage on plain paper temporarily to reduce chances of loose particles of substrate entering the healing wound. Bites from belligerent cage mates or especially ardent suitors during courtship (or unintended male-male combat) rarely are deep or serious. Their care is the same as already described for smaller open wounds after checking for any broken teeth in the wound.

Blisters and Discoloration

Blisters and discoloration may crop up between or under scales, especially the ventral plates, if the cage environment stays excessively damp for more than a few days at one time. Increased moisture allows bacteria to grow on feces, old shed skins, organic substrates, and any other nutrients that exist. Skin diseases often appear under the belly scutes first since they have the greatest contact with the floor, although they can occur anywhere on the body. The most frequent cause of persistent dampness is a tipped or overflowing water bowl.

Use only heavy bowls with vertical sides or with sides angled outward, which are less prone to tipping. Fill the bowl only halfway to minimize spillage when corn snakes coil up inside. When corns occasionally soak nonstop for many days preparatory to molting, due to an overheated cage, or to rid themselves of mites, the layers of old and new skin or active bite wounds form an ideal protected environment for bacteria to get a foothold. Remove water bowls temporarily if you see your snakes in them constantly, offering only tiny drinking basins instead. Inspect snakes thoroughly for any evidence of problems. Snakes will shed more frequently as part of the recovery process to promote faster healing after such skin problems. Applying silver sulfadiazine cream to injured areas will speed the healing. Serious injuries or excessive blistering may additionally require a herp veterinarian to prescribe a systemic antibiotic to fight infection. If topical treatment doesn't work, piperacillin has been known to be very effective in treating blister disease when given at a dosage of 80 mg/kg intramuscularly every seventy-two hours for a period of thirty days. It tends to be expensive, and not all vets keep it in stock.

Mouth Rot (Stomatitis)

As tame as corn snakes are, they don't like being confined to small shipping cups or sacks or even to cages they deem too restrictive or otherwise unsatisfactory. They explore every nook and cranny for an escape route, sometimes pushing their snouts into each one with impressive force. This, plus random nips by prey animals while being subdued, is a common cause of mouth rot.

The mouth lining and gums are quite sensitive to injury because bacterial infections thrive in moist, dark places. Typically a whitish or yellowish substance resembling cheese builds up over an infected area, causing swelling, an inability to completely close the mouth, or the formation of a scab. Most opinions favor carefully and gently removing the scab from a corn's mouth (unlike a scab on a person) using a cloth or tweezers and treating the infection daily until completely healed. This malady is quite curable but requires persistence on the keeper's part to maintain the wearisome routine. Mild cases of mouth rot may be treated topically with Listerine or a hydrogen peroxide and Betadine solution. (A 50/50 mix of hydrogen peroxide and water, then add Betadine until the color of the solution resembles weak iced tea). Apply with a cotton swab to the affected area twice daily.

NOTE: Do not apply liberal amounts of either liquid in order to avoid accidental ingestion. In more severe cases, a qualified reptile veterinarian should be consulted to run a bacterial culture and determine the appropriate antibiotic. Be aware that stomatitis can lead to infections in the mandible (jawbone), septicemia (bacteria in the bloodstream), and death. Treat this condition seriously; delayed or inconsistent treatment could be fatal.

Respiratory Disorders

Signs of respiratory disorders in *E. guttata* include many of the same symptoms as an upper respiratory disease in humans—wheezing, sneezing, mucus coming from the nostrils and mouth, breathing through the mouth instead of the nostrils, lethargy, and maybe even a rattling or gurgling feeling from within them when held. Occasionally, dry skin (or even scar tissue in some older snakes) in the nostrils will cause a false alarm because of the whistling sound it makes when the snake breathes. The sound is most often heard prior to shedding.

It is possible to treat a mild respiratory infection at home by providing a warm, dry environment. Raise the temperature to the high end of the snake's preferred temperature range, around 89°F–92°F (31.5°C–33.3°C). This is the equivalent of giving the snake an artificial fever to help it fight germs. In addition, eliminate all possible stresses on the snake including excessive handling, cage mates, and unnecessary disturbances. The sick snake should be isolated in a separate cage, and even a separate room if possible, to avoid spreading the problem.

A trip to the veterinarian for a bacterial culture and an antibiotic is recommended for more serious or stubborn cases.

Egg-binding

Occasionally a female corn fails to pass some or all of her clutch of eggs, retaining them far longer than is normal or healthy for her. An egg-binding problem is most noticeable as either an out-of-proportion or irregular bulge in a female's lower abdomen. It may also be felt as a lump or hardened mass in her body about the time you expect her to deposit her clutch or immediately afterward.

We believe that this particular problem is largely a consequence of captivity, although we suspect it could happen in nature, too. It may be that she can't find a suitable nest site in her cage when the time comes, in which case certain good mothers delay oviposition hoping to find a better site. At first she'll anxiously explore the cage at odd times until tired, possibly denting in or soiling her nose in her fervent quest. Then she rests while building the strength to try again. The remedy is obvious—put more choices of nest sites in her enclosure that are bigger, darker, moister, or drier.

After years of experience and the witnessing of literally thousands of nestings, we feel safe in surmising that a combination of lack of exercise and less-varied (but abundant) food in captive diets contributes to poorer muscle tone and the inability of some females to pass eggs naturally (dystocia). We, like many breeders who went through a large-scale commercial phase, kept our corns in cramped boxes, fed them heavily, and tried to prime them for second clutches whenever possible. Years of this regimen allowed us to watch the egg-binding phenomenon become slightly more common each season until a massive move to roomier caging eased its rate of incidence several years ago.

"Hips" are the term given to the pudgy fat deposits just above the cloaca on some older female corn snakes. The exact cause is not known—it's probably a consequence of captivity—but it doesn't necessarily impede reproduction. Snakes can remain healthy with this "blemish" for years.

We've also started a policy of offering the first pre-killed rodent of the meal (whenever we use them, which is not 100 percent of the time) from long forceps to fake the struggling of live prey so the snake constricts it upon grabbing it and thus exercises a little. Joe Hiduke informed us that the huge corn snake colony he managed was switched to a diet of more live prey than thawed frozen, and his perception is that it's a contributing factor in the frequency of dystocia decreasing noticeably. Even periodic handling (when snakes are not gravid or full of food) is a form of exercise that specimens in large collections seldom experience.

When eggs get stuck and it's determined that a female will not be passing them without help, several options exist. (An x-ray from a qualified reptile veterinarian may be warranted at this point to determine position and size.) Manual palpation may persuade the eggs to move downward. In our experience, they usually won't budge, but it's worth a quick try. DO NOT apply excessive force—this is delicate territory! Trying to move an egg from too far anterior to the cloaca may rupture the egg along the way if the egg is at all irregular. Worse, it may snag along the way and cause a portion of the oviduct to be damaged, rupture, tear, or prolapse (be expelled out the cloaca). When the egg is within about 3 inches (7.5 cm) of the cloaca, we've successfully used a slender lubricated probe gently inserted up the cloaca to encircle the egg and loosen it while also relaxing the opening itself. Careful manipulation should then be able to ease the egg out. Make sure that the probe is in contact with the egg, not the oviduct membrane, before guiding the egg out so it doesn't pull the oviduct out first.

The next effort is one that we tried experimentally about a decade ago with excellent results. Its object is to deflate the most posterior stuck egg, which we presume is the one causing the problem. Sometimes an exceptionally large, odd-shaped one gets jammed, or one gets infected or dies in utero and swells to block the others. Swabbing the skin surface adjacent to the widest point with an alcohol wipe or Betadine solution, we then aim for the stretched skin between scales. We puncture the egg from outside the body using an 18-gauge needle on a 10 cc or larger syringe. We're very careful to push the needle in only half the estimated diameter so the tip ends up in the approximate center of the egg. If the egg is accessible from the cloacal opening, we enter through that to avoid puncturing the body wall at all. Either way, a second person is necessary to securely hold the snake while this is done. The plunger is slowly withdrawn to aspirate the egg contents, repeating the procedure more than once if necessary and being very careful not to inject egg yolk into the body cavity during withdrawal of the needle. The area is again swabbed to clean it, and the snake is returned to a sterile cage for at least twenty-four hours.

Far more often than not, the remainder of the clutch is passed within a day or two. If it is only partially passed, the procedure may be repeated within a few days on the most posterior of the remaining eggs. The deflated egg(s) will look like a piece of small white balloon once passed from the female's body. Don't worry about destroying eggs—we have never discovered a fertile stuck egg, even when we were able to maneuver it undamaged through the cloaca. If you postpone acting on it for more than a week or so, the egg contents harden and aspiration often becomes impossible. Although an obvious chance for infection exists, we've never encountered it in dozens of such procedures and have gone on to breed those females in later years with good results.

Taking a different tack, an intramuscular injection of oxytocin, a drug used to induce uterine contractions in labor in women, stimulates contractions in the oviduct to get the eggs moving, although it seems to seldom work with snakes. Some breeders report success with calcium injections, but we have not tried that method ourselves.

In a really serious situation when nothing else works and the snake is becoming physically weak, true surgery is the only option left to remove an impassable clutch. A veterinarian is best sought for these last-resort methods.

IMPORTANT: Within a few days after egg deposition, check the female's entire body length carefully by hand to detect potential problems like egg retention. This is the time, when you're distracted by setting up the new clutch of eggs, that smaller, harder bad eggs may be left behind and easily missed by only a casual visual inspection of the mother.

Premature Hatching

Occasionally babies hatch early, still connected to unabsorbed remnants of their egg yolk or with a swollen, unabsorbed umbilical sack. This problem is often caused by an over-zealous keeper constantly prodding and checking the slit eggs, resulting in a nervous baby exiting the shell too soon. Isolating the baby in a deli cup with just enough clean water to cover the bottom of the cup will prevent the yolk contents from drying out or sticking to the cup bottom and rupturing. Change the water every day and keep insects from entering. The yolk should be absorbed within a couple of days.

If the hatchling manages to hatch without absorbing the yolk, but still appears normal and healthy, it will not have the stamina to wait several weeks for its first meal as its siblings might be able to do. If such a baby does not feed on its own within a couple of weeks, the keeper will have to use one of the feeding methods discussed earlier to ensure its survival.

Stress and the Unknown

Stress is still the black hole of disorders, but it's starting to catch at least partial blame these days as the cause, or at least precursor, of a multitude of maladies. We all know that nervous snakes don't act normally or feed regularly. Why shouldn't other forms of stress affect different aspects of their behavior, too, as it does in humans? The signs are usually less obvious than the straight-forward refusal of food, so it's up to us as their caretakers to observe, assess, and react to subtle indications of these problems and contribute new solutions. We certainly don't have all the answers yet, but as concerned herpetoculturists, we are interested in advancing this area of study. A few examples may help illustrate some things we've noticed so far and emphasize the importance of speculating further on this oft-neglected topic.

Our favorite culprit is the syndrome of captivity that could be dubbed limited freedom of choice. It ends up working its way into a large percentage of the answers we give to people by phone and in print. Simply summed up, most captive situations (we're including the bulging ranks of people new at keeping corn snakes in our assessment) do not offer the voluntary range of daily environmental choices available in the wild. Snakes can't warm up or cool down quickly by moving in or out of the sun to change body temperature. This severely affects their natural ability to digest food optimally, to hamper diseases or parasites by exposing them to extremes (such as when our bodies create fever conditions), or to regulate other hormonal functions that we haven't yet investigated. Their choice of wetness or dryness (we mean ambient conditions, not merely having drinking water available or not) may aid in shedding cleanly or curing fungal infections. Having a truly safe retreat for those times when snakes prefer to shut down all activity levels and avoid disturbance (for instance, while digesting a prodigious meal, while in shed, or at egg deposition time) may be more necessary than we suspect. Complex hormonal functions may require total relaxation and privacy to proceed in an orderly fashion for the next phase of their bodies' physiological needs. Even the vibrations bouncing through an active household, and ultimately their cages, may leave snakes in a constant state of minor agitation because it's an instinct to take heed of such signals as potential danger.

Our love of convenience often dictates offering a monotonously unvarying diet of domestic rodents to our charges. Is it unreasonable to think that wild corns sometimes take to the trees to specifically seek avian prey for a change of pace, analogous to the cravings of pregnant women for unusual foods? Maybe corns even occasionally revert to their youthful diet of frogs or lizards when their bodies tell them to seek a needed dose of vitamins or minerals they lack. In captivity they also lose whatever benefit they may derive from trace minerals ingested in the guts of natural wild prey. Can this be of greater long-term significance than anyone currently suspects? Even the mere lack of exercise in pursuit of these needs may in itself be stressful.

Change of any kind is stressful, even a change for the better. Moving your snake into a new cage or even moving the old cage to a new location requires some adjustment time before expecting normal feeding and handling. Some animals, just like some humans, are more resilient than others. The stress of acquiring a new animal—shipping or transporting it home—and setting it up in completely new conditions contributes even more stress than moving it around your home. Oblivious new owners often bring home a new snake, handle it, show it to their friends, put it in the new cage, and then toss in a mouse to watch it eat. This is asking a lot of a scared new pet!

The quality of our heavily treated city water supplies may be slowly poisoning our snakes with an accumulation of trace elements that they, as small-bodied organisms, have lower tolerances for than humans. Cage water also tends to sit for long spells, weeks if we use conveniently oversize bowls that don't empty quickly, creating a stagnant pool in which pathogens can multiply, protected from sun, rain, and wind that would normally sterilize, dilute, or dry up a water source.

An even more common place offense is our controlling the timing of light our animals live under to suit our whim. Who isn't guilty of casually flipping on the lights at some odd hour to check something, or worse yet, pulling the snake out from cover to show a visitor? What would your reaction to such an intrusion be at 3:00 a.m. when you were sound asleep? Since we know that most animals and plants are still far more closely linked to the natural photoperiods that govern their life cycles than are people, such disruptions could critically affect the fine-tuning of the biological clocks snakes may depend upon for normal daily life.

The quality of light may also be an important factor we've thus far dismissed as insignificant. We know from human tests that the effects of unnatural tones of light, as are emitted by most incandescent and fluorescent bulbs, affect peoples' moods and productivity. We already know that ultraviolet components of sunlight are essential for some other herp species to properly metabolize elements of their diets. For species so heavily influenced by the one and only source of light that forever dominates their lives, the sun, is it unreasonable to assume that altering its intensity or wavelength spectrum will have some effect?

Murkier realms exist. Pollution from agricultural and industrial chemicals, hormones, and poisons have created a worrisome new area of scientific concern: endocrine disruption. Complicated biological processes like embryonic development are being distorted by exposure to even traces of substances entering the environment. Altering just one link in the precise chain of events in an organism's growth can spell doom. What could ultrasonic communications frequencies that now reverberate across our planet be doing to unknown snake senses needed in migration, finding mates, or evaluating changing weather? Could we be causing a short circuit in the finely tuned sensory systems of many lower life-forms without even being conscious of the disruption because our own limited senses are (apparently) not affected adversely? We present these thoughts to inspire deeper examination of the complexities of life and how we may be unwittingly affecting them for our captives and ourselves.

CHAPTER 7

COLOR AND PATTERN VARIATIONS

Showy colors are what first attract most people to corn snakes as pets. Then people realize the myriad variations corn snakes can display and that anyone can easily manipulate these traits in successive captive generations. It's like the latent artist in us all finding a new format to explore, using a canvas that already fascinates us. Moreover, if intrinsic beauty isn't enough to entice us, the prospect of monetary reward from breeding success looms on a not-too-distant horizon.

The naturally occurring races of *E. guttata* were covered briefly in the introduction. What wasn't really elaborated upon was the tremendous range of natural color variation within particular subspecies and even among individuals of local populations. No photo, or even dozens of them, can completely prepare you for what the next specimen may

The variety of colors and patterns in *Elaphe guttata* seems limited only by breeders' imaginations.

Not all corns are ravishing beauties! This is a completely average-looking specimen of corn snake collected in southern Florida. Note the "dirty wash" of melanin muddying the colors, a trait that's common on many large corns living in the wild.

look like. This point is often missed by inexperienced individuals trying to key out species in a field guide that emphasizes picture identifications. It also causes misunderstandings when people have the tendency to lock onto a favorite image of a nice-looking corn in a book or magazine. People forget about variation and the fact that photographers are strongly motivated to shoot the most attractive subjects possible in order to sell their photos. Hobbyists assume they can order a snake that looks just like one in the picture on the price list. Spending a day people-watching at the mall will make this lesson obvious as you try to think of a way to describe the average human being. If you've ever rated members of the opposite sex on a scale of

Specimens from the Okeetee region have long been hailed as the quintessential beauties of the corn snake world. Bold black and white ventral patterns are one of their trademark features along with bright, high-contrast dorsal coloration.

145

one to ten, you know the range of differences is undeniable and often a source of great interest or desire. The analogy translates well to corn snakes. All field guides showing corn snakes face the so-far insurmountable dilemma of depicting what's in the wild with the limited number of photos that can be allowed to represent each species. Since no two corns look exactly alike, your experience will forever be limited to the chosen few that end up in print and to the ones you're able to see alive. Don't despair—this is good and exciting news! It means that the guttata universe is still expanding, and there's plenty of room for everyone to participate in its continuing cultivation and evolution. In this chapter we'll discuss all known color and pattern traits in corns. To paint a backdrop before delving into them and the genetics of variations, we'll first examine the naturally occurring corn snake morphs that are frequently seen today.

Hatchling corns have yet to develop their normal complement of yellow that later provides their beautiful range of orange tones. The two Okeetee corns shown are full siblings one year apart in age, clearly demonstrating the phenomenon of ontogenetic color change.

Naturally Occurring Corn Morphs

Average *E. guttata* specimens have a row of thirty to fifty large square or rectangular blotches running down the midline of their backs. The first blotch is usually connected to a spearhead-shaped marking atop the head, and the last one is virtually at the tail's tip. A second set of smaller and more irregularly shaped markings alternates with the dorsal blotches along the sides, although the lateral blotches vary

A typical adult corn snake from the Okeetee area of South Carolina shows that not all specimens from that area are like the "10s" being selectively bred today.

tremendously in size, shape, and exact placement. All these blotches have black or dark outlines of varying thicknesses and centers of some shade of red, orange, brown, or some combination of these colors. The ground color between blotches may be any shade of yellow to orange-red, or it may lean toward a light to dark gray or tan. The wide belly scales (ventral scutes) may be white, yellow, red, or orange and are usually marked with a series of roughly geometrical shapes in contrasting black. All these traits are subject to alteration over relatively short periods of time (one to three years per generation on average) through selective breeding, which is one reason why corns are such popular study species for ongoing herpetocultural projects.

Okeetee Corn

This is the quintessentially ultimate normal corn snake, encompassing all the traits that people love in the species as a whole. Carl Kauffeld popularized this big, husky "race" in two books about snake hunting. The name was bestowed in honor of the property on which Kauffeld and associates first collected them for the Staten Island Zoo's collection in New York, the Okeetee Club. The Okeetee Club is a 50,000-acre private hunting preserve in Jasper County, South Carolina, that is not open to the public for snake hunting.

The name Okeetee has withstood the test of time and become the designation for classically beautiful corns from coastal southern South Carolina. Collectors have since descended upon the region annually, especially in the spring, to experience the thrill of field collecting that renowned hot spot for ultra-gorgeous corn snakes. An Okeetee is not a separate subspecies or even a well-defined race of corn snake; it's simply a designation for southern South Carolina's pretty corns that has stuck to promote a tie to that "historic" area.

For the record, virtually all the land in the region is private property now. Simply hopping out of the car "at a spot that looks snakey" and traipsing off with sack and field hook in hand isn't an option anymore like it was back in the good ol' days when landowners weren't fed up with trespassing snake hunters.

Okeetee corn snakes include, but are not limited to, individuals with deep red dorsal blotches ringed by well-defined, jet-black borders. The ground color ranges from russet to bright orange and is contrasted clearly and cleanly by the distinctive black. Two dorsal and two lateral hazy dark stripes, more prominent on some individuals than

This high-contrast Okeetee corn epitomizes the ideal breeders strive for. Clean, exquisitely colored creatures like this remain perennial favorites, even with the heavy competition of numerous beautiful aberrant morphs.

others, may appear over the blotches for the length of the body. The belly has a prominent squarish black checkerboard pattern covering it, and it tends to have a white ground color for most of its length. The ventral scutes may also have some orange between the checkering, especially toward the latter half of the body.

It is now known that attractive corns fitting this general description inhabit the entire Atlantic Coastal Plain from eastern North Carolina down into northeastern Florida. More importantly, and often neglected in the fervor to find the most exquisite example, not every animal from the Okeetee region is a classic beauty. Some are very ordinary in looks, and a few are rather dull and unremarkable. However, after years of selective breeding, typical captive Okeetee corns are often stunningly colored compared to average specimens of *E. guttata*. This fact has unfortunately been exploited occasionally to help sell normal, undifferentiated hatchlings or offspring diluted from Okeetee stock crossed to something else, since the Okeetee name has become synonymous with the stunning coloration many collectors seek. The amount of orange coloration attained by the adult is not easily judged in very young examples.

Miami Phase

The name for this morph is derived from specimens commonly found in the agricultural areas south and west of Miami, Florida, around which *E. guttata* occurs in high densities. Miami phase corns typically display a silvery-gray background color with various amounts of orange dusting or speckling mixed into it, although not all examples adhere very closely to the standard we've described. The dorsal blotch color is generally more orange than red, often with whitish spots or pale centers, especially toward the sides. At its best, with the ground color and dorsal blotches appearing as pure, even tones, this morph resembles a light phase gray-banded king snake, *Lampropeltis alterna*. In reality, most snakes exhibit flaws in the smoothness or uniformity of the gray and orange. Hatchlings from this area often tend to average a little smaller in size than other strains of corns,

Corns from extreme southeastern Florida often look like this one. Grey background colors are the norm, but its "purity" and the contrast between it and the orange-red blotch color may be unremarkable.

and a small but significant percentage prefer lizards, especially anoles, instead of pink mice for their first meals. Once started, they are no different from any other corn. Adults can grow as large as more northern corns, but Miami phase corns are often smaller, averaging only 3–4 feet (91–122 cm) in length.

It's not uncommon for corns in other areas of their range to show up with gray ground colors. It's important to note that this trait is not restricted only to southern Florida specimens. Some breeders may carefully restrict their Miami phase corn colonies to Miami-Dade County specimens, but many breeders have outcrossed them (bred them to totally unrelated corns to avoid inbreeding depression—the tendency for inbred strains to weaken over time due to a buildup of undesirable recessive genes) into a variety of other colors and patterns. This practice has resulted in a higher percentage of good feeders and more variability in color and pattern. If such information is important to you, be sure to ask the breeder about the heritage of his or her animals.

Rich Zuchowski has developed a variant dubbed milk snake phase. It is essentially an enhanced Miami phase corn in which some examples exhibit very uniform blotching on a clean grayish-white background. The milk snake phase resemblance to certain cleanly patterned milk snakes (*Lampropeltis triangulum*) formed the basis of the name for this intensified version of an old favorite.

The Hatband Test

From the preceding accounts, it should be plain that any variation could become the next "new" captive morph with some selective breeding effort. It merely takes somebody to notice a standout specimen with unusual or appealing traits that might be reliably reproduced and preferably accentuated, or even exaggerated. Since there are no official rules about naming color or pattern variants, as exist in scientific circles when describing species, new names have only to stand the "market test" for a few years to determine if their creation is distinct in the eyes of the public. Memorable names hit the pet trade every year—just look at the trend in ball python *Python regius* marketing. These are attempts to draw curiosity and attention. With corns, using colorful, tasty food names like *creamsicle*, *butter*, and *candycane*, for instance, are more than just descriptive. They invoke imagination and desire, a *hunger*, for those animals.

Ultimately a second trait—long-term desirability—will decide if a variant can withstand the test of time. If it does, it will remain available as a recognized morph that hobbyists and breeders preserve through captive breeding. With snakes, we've coined this phenomenon "passing the hatband test," referencing both the usage of snake skins as decorations on cowboy hats, and comparing it to the potential lasting power of clothes fashions, which depend on the breadth and endurance of their visual appeal. Essentially, if a new corn snake's color and/or pattern makes an eye-catching decoration if worn like an exotic hatband (we frown on killing any snake for this reason, of course), it will have broad appeal to the general public.

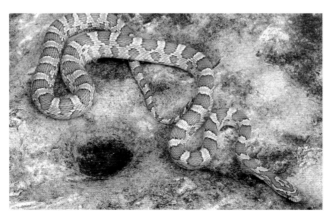

Breeders work to "improve" typical Miami phase corns by emphasizing clean blotch and background colors.

Genetics

B-o-r-i-n-g! You may be tempted to think, I'd better move on to the pictures because this is bound to be complicated. Besides, I can always call the breeder and ask what I'll get if I cross a green-blotched snow-stripe with a ghost motley heterozygous for albinism. We're acutely aware of the difficulty people have with genetics and are trying to make it as simple as possible in the section that follows. Mainly we'll concentrate on what happens, especially regarding simple dominant vs. recessive genetics, and let you proceed to an academic biology text for most of the fine details of the hows and whys of the complex stuff.

The Internet also offers help in this area, but the list of Web sites with new information about genetics and corn snake morphs increases every year and is impossible to keep current on paper. In addition, many sites change uniform resource locators (URLs) with maddening regularity. We will continue to update our own Web site located at http://www.cornutopia.com with links to interesting sites that are discovered offering significant new information and pictures about corn snakes. Check our links section for this ever-evolving list. Also, check out this book's appendix about how to reach Web sites that offer specific help that will take much of the guesswork out of predicting hatch ratios of most forms of recessive color and pattern mutations.

Many popular corn snake color variations are not merely normal or extra nice versions of morphs currently found in nature. They appeared when a recessive gene was paired with another copy of itself in a single snake, and that snake fell into a breeder's hands. Amelanism (regular albinism) is the classic example; it was the first morph and multiplied geometrically to propel herpetoculture and corn snakes to where they are today.

Odd new recessive traits are showing up with much greater frequency than just a decade or two ago for two good reasons. The first is due to the booming popularity of herp keeping. More people are in the field catching wild herps for the pet trade. Not only are more corn snakes being caught, but more gravid females are collected proportionately, dropping their eggs to hatch in captivity. Spurred by the contemporary widespread employment of captive-breeding techniques to proliferate traits that please us, those hunters are keeping an extra sharp eye peeled for any individuals, caught by or hatching for them, that sport a slightly different look. They know that people are ready and willing to pay a premium price for the chance to work with something new, especially if it may net them future profits.

New genes often alter animals so that they are not as fit for survival in the wild as are the normal-looking types. Abnormally colored specimens may be easier for predators to find and eat, as with amelanistics, which do not blend into the natural background but rather glow against it. The amelanistic's lack of pigmentation also makes it more vulnerable to harmful solar rays. These individuals usually perish as juveniles without ever being seen by humans.

The second reason for an increased frequency of recessive traits, as opposed to dominant traits, is the nature of recessive genes. In corn snakes, as in humans, genes exercise their control over phenotypes (appearances) in pairs, with one of each pair received from each parent. If both parents contribute a normal gene for a trait, then the baby shows the normal trait. If one parent passes a normal gene, and a recessive abnormal gene is inherited from the other parent (such as one of the pair needed to cause the lack of black pigment in corns), then the babies still show the normal trait. The single recessive gene is masked by the dominant gene for black that alone can oversee the normal production of that pigment. Babies carrying the genes for a recessive trait but not showing that trait are heterozygous, which literally means having a pair of nonidentical genes, a mixed genetic heritage, concerning a particular trait. It is the opposite of homozygous, the state in which both genes governing a single trait are identical. The term heterozygous is often shortened to hetero or just "het" on dealers' and breeders' price lists.

When recessive genes result in a different, abnormal appearance in a corn snake, such as amelanism, it's because those recessive genes exist in a paired homozygous state. If even one of the gene pair is for the normal (dominant) look with black pigment, it dominates the trait and negates any influence of the recessive gene. Recessive genes must be in a homozygous state to exert their effect.

Recessive genes are more likely to get paired in small groups of animals, like captive colonies in which related individuals breed together and share gene pools, than in large populations of unrelated ones that have strangers carrying fresh genes moving in and out haphazardly. Animals in a collection, especially after a couple of generations of successful matings (and holding back of future breeding stock from the offspring produced), tend to share much more genetic material than any random group of specimens in the field. Consequently, like genes are paired more frequently, and new recessive traits pop up relatively more often in captivity than in free-roaming wild populations. When it happens in nature, the new mutation offers the population a potential boost that might let it take advantage of new conditions and prove to be beneficial in the long run. If it doesn't improve survival chances, and most of the fancy traits we admire do not, few individuals are wasted in the "experiment," and those showing the trait die off before becoming old enough to pass on their genes. The opposite holds true in captive populations where corns expressing new traits are highly valued. These are nurtured and have an increased chance of surviving. This difference in selection pressure causes the wild and captive gene pools to slowly creep away from each other with each successive generation.

Many aspiring breeders have been warned to avoid inbreeding (mating animals closely related to one another in their family ancestry) their captive herps if possible, but they don't really know why. The simplest explanation is that inbreeding concentrates traits, good and bad, within family lines. This increases the likelihood that undesirable traits will show up after two carriers of those genes mate. Hidden recessive traits probably exist in many individuals, those traits lurking in a heterozygous state. They'll tend to get paired with similar recessive genes in other corns and be able to show themselves sooner when more potential mates in the vicinity also carry the gene. Traits that would be disadvantageous in the wild, such as the many mutations in corn snakes that affect skin colors and patterns, are harmless and even desirable in the safety of captivity. However, undesirable traits, such as kinked spines and deformed scales and eyes, also show up. Breeders must select their stock carefully, culling out animals with physical deformities and breeding only those specimens exhibiting solely the desirable and nonharmful traits.

The mixing of various color and pattern traits has become a favorite pastime among hobbyists. Fortunately this combats inbreeding depression. Common effects of inbreeding depression syndrome are shorter body lengths, lower weights, eye defects, lower egg and clutch sizes, skeletal imperfections, and infertility. Crossing unrelated corns to bring in new traits also refreshes all the hidden recessive genes that were accumulating after successive generations of inbreeding efforts. This process, the phenomenon of hybrid vigor, is common, even essential, in the wild to maintain healthy populations. In nature, it is accomplished through the long-range wanderings of male corn snakes as they seek mates further afield in spring.

At the same time, we also mustn't rule out the possibility that bizarre physical anomalies may purposely be striven for in the not-so-distant future. A hatchling corn showing an aberration might be dismissed as undesirable by 99 percent of us and immediately destroyed, but it takes only one person to nurture such a mutant and perpetuate its characteristics while turning the gross defect into a unique selling point. This kind of situation currently exists in the line of pure white (leucistic) Texas rat snakes, *E. obsoleta lindheimeri*, some of which inherit a bug-eyed enlargement of the eyes. Most people consider it an ugly negative attribute to be avoided, few people believe that it does the snakes any harm and are working to accentuate the trait.

Genetic Color Mutations

Amelanism

Also known as albino (albinistic), amel, or red albino, the proper name for the trait that means "without black pigment" is amelanistic. The confusion in these terms arises from the fact that the word albino is derived from the Latin word *albus*, meaning white. It was applied to the condition in humans where melanin, our only pigment, was absent. This mutation is one of the most occurring in nature in all kinds of vertebrate animals, but the old assumption that it results in a white animal, as it does in mammals, doesn't apply to reptiles with their several different skin pigments. Corn snakes also have red and yellow pigments and a layer of cells in their skins called iridophores or reflective cells that are responsible for the whites, prismatic luster, and other subtle tones of the other colors. Taking black away from corn snakes leaves dazzling color, which often appears brighter than normal without the overcoating of melanin. The multitude of colors complicates the genetics but allows a much greater array of color combinations to occur when mixing and matching genes. A neonate's yellow pigmentation develops during the first several months after hatching, further muddying the immediate prediction of adult coloration. Take heart—those dark reddish-brown babies will improve steadily and quickly.

Amelanistic corns have been phenomenally popular as pets due to their bright colors. Note that they are mainly only red and white at hatching until yellow pigment develops and fills in over the first year of life.

The elimination of all white flecks, leaving only reds and oranges, is the goal when breeding sunglow amelanistic corns.

The various shades of red, yellow, black, and white combine in amelanistic corn snakes in a multitude of ways, depending, of course, on the appearance of the original normal ancestors. Particularly significant are how prevalent each color was in them and exactly where it was distributed over their bodies. In the early to mid-1980s, herpetoculturists started to focus on more than just indiscriminately breeding more amelanistic corns. We and a couple of other people began to selectively breed specimens that already showed some promise of extreme or unusual coloration, much as has been done with the normal corns discussed earlier.

One of the most popular strains today exhibits blotches that range from deep red to red-orange on a clean, slightly lighter orange background with very little or no white speckling. The earliest animals we obtained in our own work on this variation trace back to Norm Damm in Ohio, and ultimately to Vince Scheidt in California. Over several more generations, we and other breeders were able to select the characteristics to obtain the consistent colors seen in most of today's specimens. We originally called this morph no-white albino, but we changed it later to the more memorable (and salable) sunglow.

Our coining of that unusual cultivar in *E. guttata* helped set off a trend that has flourished. It has propelled widespread adoption of the practice as thousands of private

Albino Okeetee corns look like amelanistic versions of normal Okeetee corns in which the wide black dorsal blotch rings are reversed to white.

herpetoculturists now participate in similar selective breeding projects and the subsequent marketing of the progeny. Various efforts are underway to intensify the red aspect with the addition of bloodred corn bloodlines that should eventually fuse those traits into one incredibly brilliant red corn snake morph. Others are attempting to breed the no-white color coverage into primarily yellow creamsicle and butter corns, with the goal of achieving a real dazzler with deep red blotches on a glowing yellow background.

During the mid- to late 1980s, we noticed that a few specimens in our colony possessed unusually large white borders around the blotches and singled them out for a special project. One particular snake beauty from Mike and Linda Krick had a special flair toward that trait. As more offspring accumulated in our colony, we remarked how some of those attractive animals were reminiscent of classic Okeetee corns, only with white replacing the usual black outlining of the blotches. They still provided the same pleasing contrast, with even more brilliant colors because of the lack of black. The ground color was distinctly lighter yellowish-orange than the blotch tone, which provided additional contrast. Naturally, we started looking for and selectively breeding for this trait, especially trying to breed for ever-wider white rings. Subsequently, other corns were crossed in when they exhibited some characteristic that might heighten the effect. It was not necessary that all were descended from Okeetee stock since the emphasis was on appearance, not heritage. They became known first as the reverse Okeetee and later as the albino Okeetee corn snake, based on looks alone.

Concurrently, Glen Slemmer of Vancouver, British Columbia, was crossing Great Plains rat snakes (*E. guttata emoryi*) with amelanistic corns to increase the amount of yellow pigment and to decrease the red, hoping to create a golden yellow-orange variation of corn. The resulting subspecific crosses can range from golden yellow to, more often, an orange-butterscotch color. The one constant is that they lack any real red. True to their emoryi roots, clutch sizes tend to be smaller than those of pure corns, but the babies are often larger and more robust and are easy to get started feeding on newborn mice. These snakes were named creamsicles presumably due to their pastel-orange coloring resembling a popular frozen dessert on a stick. That silly-sounding moniker may be one of the reasons it has become a well-remembered favorite to this day in the pet trade. The normal-colored crosses from *guttata* and *emoryi* crossings have become known as root beer corns.

The goal of the creamsicle project has been realized in a different way: the amelanistic Emory's rat snake—a new strain pioneered by Don Soderberg and only reproduced for the first time in the late 1990s. We have dubbed this new gene amel2 to distinguish it from the old established form, which we'll continue to refer to as simply amel. We predict that amel2 will soon be crossed and mixed thoroughly with other lines of *E. guttata* to display all sorts of new color combinations of yellow and red in a vast replay of the aims of the original creamsicle project and beyond.

There are downsides to mixing amel2 with other corns exhibiting or carrying genes for the original amel gene. One is that the two types of amelanism are not genetically compatible—amel and amel2 genes brought together in offspring via crosses lending one form of amelanistic gene from each parent do not combine in a homozygous state to result in individuals lacking black. So, future amelanistic

This spectacular albino Okeetee has taken the white blotch borders to the extreme, and eliminated the yellow in the ground color too, as has also been the goal of candycane corn breeding.

corns will exhibit or be heterozygous for both types of amelanism. Since they will probably be indistinguishable from each other, hobbyists will be frustrated when breeding two amels together only to get non-amel offspring or some normals and some unidentifiable amels.

Another pitfall is that purists do not want mixtures of pure corns and anything else, especially now that *E. guttata emoryi* is being regarded as a full species by some people. As soon as creamsicles become part of the recipe for other combos, the ancestry may be lost. It is therefore very important to keep accurate records of the pedigrees in your colony and to always properly describe them when selling or giving away offspring.

The amount of background yellow can vary, affecting the looks of adult corns tremendously. These are both albino Great Plains rat snakes.

Candycanes are a fourth cultivar of the amelanistic corn. Ideally, a candycane is a whitish snake with bright red-orange blotches. They were developed by Glen Slemmer and later named and refined by Kevin Enge by crossing selected adults with little background color between the dorsal blotches. Miami phase corn bloodlines with clean light gray areas between the blotches contributed some of the original stock, as did some *E. g. emoryi* specimens with pale backgrounds, creamsicles, and other amelanistics in other peoples' efforts to perfect them. This color phase has proven to be difficult to produce reliably, and only recently have babies with really white backgrounds become readily available. A number of breeders worked independently to produce candycanes, so some lines will have slightly different "ingredients," or genetic backgrounds, than do other lines.

Because corns gain yellow pigment as they age, babies of all strains often have the look of a candycane, but later blossom out with yellows and oranges in the ground color. Therefore, it is extremely difficult to predict which babies will show the most highly contrasting whitish backgrounds as adults. In refining the candycane strain, serious breeders always hold on to many more babies than they really want for at least six to twelve months to determine which ones to keep permanently. It's the only reliable way to improve breeding colonies whose ultimate appearance is a product of

Candycane corns are bred to resemble their namesakes with only bright red (or orange) blotches against as pure of a white ground color as possible.

Fluorescent aptly describes this morph of amelanistic corn that concentrates on the brilliance of the red-orange background color. The wide white blotch borders to make it stand out in a crowd.

slow individual changes during maturation. Keep this fact in mind when purchasing hatchlings of this and other strains; even the breeders can't always pick the very best ones at extremely early ages when developing yellow will play a key role in adult appearance.

A fifth variant has been named fluorescent orange. It originated with a pair of sibling amelanistic snakes, the female of which Rich Zuchowski felt showed a hint of piebaldism when it hatched in 1987. Fluorescent orange corns resemble bright albino Okeetee corns in many ways. Random white splotching has not yet reappeared in subsequent offspring, but the white bordering the dorsal blotches is extra wide and bold, and the ground color between the blotches is an unusually vibrant orange.

Anerythrism

Also known confusingly as melanistic, anerythristic, anery, type A anerythrism, and black albino, a corn with anerythrism possesses a recessive genetic defect that leaves it unable to form red and most yellow pigments, similar to the way amelanistics lack black. Superficially it resembles the gray rat snake (*E. obsoleta spiloides*), Emory's rat snake, or a black-and-white or sepia-tone picture of a typical corn snake. Grays, browns, and blacks predominate in an otherwise normal pattern of blotches. No other color is evident except traces of yellow on the lower throat, chin, and labial (lip) areas, and these traces may be formed by a separate accumulation of carotenoids (red and yellow pigments often contained in natural foods).

It's also possible that the residual yellow may develop as an actual bodily function that produces yellow pigment by a secondary or backup system. Maybe it's only supposed to add an extra touch of yellow on the throat and labials for reasons we haven't yet determined and still does so even when it's the only yellow-producing system working at the

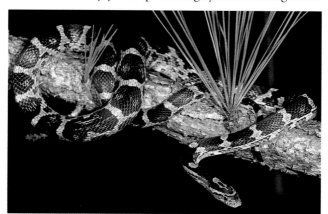

Type A anerythristic corns lack all red pigmentation, and most yellow too. The yellow that is present is usually concentrated on the chin and throat areas of mature animals.

time. Either of these suggestions might also explain the tendency in some big anerythristics to fade into a dull brown with advanced age. Many older snakes take on very meager amounts of reds or yellows that muddy the higher-contrast black-on-white of their youths. There must be a mechanism, such as gradual gain through dietary sources, that installs normal corn snake pigments in these older individuals. This means there may be more than one way to achieve the creation of pigments when the primary systems are cancelled genetically by the recessive mutations we've all gotten used to regarding as all-or-nothing traits.

Type A anerythrism has turned up many times in wild populations. It's not uncommon to find one adorning the road at dusk in the Immokalee Triangle, an area roughly between the three cities of Immokalee, Ft. Myers, and Moore Haven in southwestern Florida. Local people see them often enough to call them gray rat snakes; true gray rat

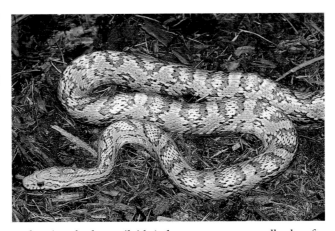

This anery corn has extreme yellow, making it highly attractive over the typical specimen that is generally lacking in showy colors. It may also be a result of hybridization with *Elaphe obsoleta*, which could alternately account for its appearance.

snakes (*E. obsoleta spiloides*) do not occur naturally that far south in Florida. The deficit of red hasn't seemed to unduly burden their chances at survival because they appear to be getting more common. It's not clear yet if this trend may be falsely enhanced by more snake hunters collecting from the region in recent decades. The vast majority of wild-caught specimens from southwestern Florida that lack red pigment are the common type A anerythrism. This type helped create virtually all the other early combination morphs that lack red and yellow pigment, including snow corns and ghost corns.

A stonewashed morph of anerythrism (with a faded appearance that mimics the effect of new denim jeans laundered with smooth stones to achieve a weathered look) was marketed for awhile, but the name is seldom used anymore. There may additionally be a second subtle color- or pattern-related gene influencing this look, or it may just be a variation in normal anerythrism that hasn't been widely seen or appreciated yet. (See the brief discussion of what may be a related strain, the frosted corn, further on.)

For years, having one form of anerythrism that was inherited in the standard recessive manner left it relatively easy to predict offspring from matings involving this trait. Then we stumbled upon a second kind of anerythrism in 1984 when we purchased an unusual-looking 2-foot-long (61 cm) female that reputedly came from Pine Island, a coastal island of Lee County, Florida. She lacked the yellow found in the neck area of other specimens, and the basic color was a muted, silvery gray, lacking the usual brownish-yellow cast and not showing as much contrast as a typical anery corm. It was not a very flashy or astounding difference, but we noticed it because we were actively seeking anything new in the dealers' shops during those years. Although we did not see any yellow on that original female, charcoal corns have proven that they can produce yellows, making it more difficult to distinguish between charcoals and the original anerythristics.

When this Pine Island female produced both anerythristic and normal offspring when bred to corns of type A anerythrism and snow, we felt that we had discovered some kind of new gene. Normal colored offspring should not have been possible if her anerythrism had been the same as the type A anerythrism of the male that bred her. Two parent corns exhibiting the same recessive trait (assuming that they aren't both also heterozygous for other traits) are only supposed to be able to give rise to more of the same. After a few further breeding trials, we finally concluded that she not only exhibited a new gene, type B anerythrism, but also that she was a carrier for the more common type A as well. The newer strain was previously called muted, but the designation of charcoal has gained favor and replaced it as the accepted cultivar or trade name. Hatchlings are unique in having a faint bluish cast to

This is the original Pine Island female, which later proved to be charcoal or type B anerythristic.

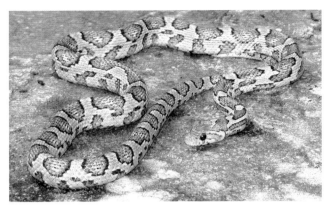

The charcoal corn is the B form of anerythrism. This one lacks even the hints of yellow on the chin and throat of type As, but some type Bs do have a little yellow.

the eyes and head scales that sets them apart from type A anerythristics in the litter.

Variation exists among black albinos as within all corn morphs, making some of them contrast highly when endowed with well-differentiated black blotches and pale grayish-white ground colors. The adjective pastel is catching on as a prefix name for certain specimens, especially among ghosts and light-colored anerythristic motleys, whenever a significant amount of pinkish-orange coloration develops between their blotches.

We've seen some very dark specimens overall, but none so uniformly black as to be deemed melanistic (a condition in which melanin dominates the appearance, covering a larger than normal percentage of the body). In theory, a truly melanistic corn should strongly resemble a black rat snake (*E. obsoleta obsoleta*) or black racer (*Coluber constrictor*). Something leaning well in the melanistic direction was found in Kansas a few years ago and has been dubbed chocolate Emory's by Don Soderberg. He has already proven its heavy brown wash to be genetically recessive and will soon be mixing and matching it to explore the possibilities with other morphs.

Hypomelanism
So far we've discussed all-or-nothing traits like amelanism in which either the color is present or it is not. The amount of melanin in corns is also influenced by genes that are

This chocolate emoryi is as close as we've seen to true melanism in *Elaphe guttata*.

responsible for the amount of dirty wash and the solidity and density of black in all parts of the pattern. The normal tendency is for great variation to exist in these traits among natural populations of corns, such as those in the lower Florida Keys that are generally light-colored with ill-defined blotch borders. Melanin also increases with age in corns, which is why larger, older specimens tend to get uglier (darker) than when they were in their prime at about 2 feet (61 cm) long. Even between siblings, though, the range of black in evidence can be startling. Any corn having reduced melanin compared to the last one you saw could be described as hypomelanistic. This is not what we're talking about when we discuss hypomelanism below.

As the emerging herpetocultural hobby grew, people started looking carefully for other mutations that might add to the palette of colors and patterns that could be manipulated through selective breeding. One simple recessive trait that has shown up in corns as well as other species is the genetically recessive reduction of black pigment–hypomelanism (later called "Hypo A" as other forms of hypomelanism became recognized), as we'll refer to it from this point on. We first became aware of it in the mid-1980s from an animal displayed at George Van Horn's Reptile World in St. Cloud, Florida. We obtained offspring and eventually reproduced it ourselves through the same strategy as was described for amelanism. John Cole also stumbled onto a strain of it from the Tampa, Florida, region

The bronzing or fading of the black in this hypo corn's saddle rings and ventral checkerboarding clearly show the effects of hypomelanism.

and was experimenting with it at the same time. Our efforts joined forces soon afterward through the exchange of specimens.

Although the eyes retain some pigment, they are lighter than the eyes of normal corns but remain darker than the pink eyes of amelanistic corns. The distribution of black pigment is reduced both dorsally and ventrally over the rest of the body. The intensity of the remaining melanin itself is lessened differentially across individuals, often turning black areas anywhere from a chocolate brown or bronze tone to making them fade away almost completely. Darker hypomelanstic individuals can often be identified by studying the quality of the dark pigment under a bright light. The dark colors may appear completely black at first

Another presumed hypo has been dubbed "Christmas corn." Its ancestry can be traced to a few specimens from Daufuskie Island, South Carolina. Early breedings point toward it being a distinct genetic form of hypomelanism.

glance but usually are really a charcoal bronze instead of a true black. The degree of black reduction in turn affects the brilliance of the underlying colors.

Hypomelanistic (also called hypo and rosy) corns can be at least as attractive as amelanistics because the remaining dark color provides interesting contrast to the cleaned-up, often intense, reds and yellows. As hatchlings they are easily distinguished from normal corns in the same clutch by their overall brighter look. The strain we've bred for more than a decade is clearly inherited as a simple recessive trait, although natural variation still exerts itself on each individual to make the range of differences virtually as great as among normal corns.

In an effort to explore its brightening potential, breeders have crossed hypomelanism into virtually every known line of corns. Don Soderberg has created a spectacular variant on the basic Miami phase theme by introducing the hypomelanistic gene to make what he calls the hypo Miami. Rich Zuchowski used the same mix to create crimson corns, which has more red-orange and less of the gray background than the hypo Miami. Hypomelanism may also be at the root of the odd effect seen on frosted corns.

We also suspect that hypoxanthism, in which the normal reds and/or yellows are reduced but not totally eliminated, probably exists already and just hasn't been recognized as such yet. Collectors are now looking for such less obvious anomalies with greater interest as the idea of selective breeding is more widely understood and used to create the astounding number of new cultivars showing up each year.

In recent years, hypomelanism has become a whole new can of worms to understand and predict. First, a new type of hypo gene turned up in our own collection of pure Okeetees in the 1990s. It looked very similar to the old hypo, except that the individuals had Okeetee patterns and colors with less than the usual amount of black. It has since been dubbed hypo Okeetee or sunkissed (also Sunkist, or "Hypo B") Okeetee. Rich Zuchowski was the first to breed the two types together and produce all normals, proving them to be separate genes.

Unfortunately, some specimens from this bloodline carry what is an associated problem gene that may also be inherited recessively, with or without the new hypo effect. The deformity, dubbed stargazing, only affects some of the babies in a clutch, often about one-fourth of them as would be expected in a recessive trait from het parents. Immediately after hatching, the affected neonates exhibit deficiencies in motor abilities. Often appearing normal at rest, they move erratically, often bending the neck and forepart of the body at odd angles, sometimes crawling upside down. Such babies are assumed to have inherited both recessive genes for this trait and are euthanized. The normal clutch mates may or may not be carrying the trait, but none so far have ever exhibited any problem associated with the trait themselves. Eventually, careful test breedings, record keeping, and elimination of proven carriers from the

Hypo corns are easily distinguished from normal corns as hatchlings when the reduced black lets the hypo baby "shine" next to its normal sibling.

breeding colony will result in elimination of this deleterious gene. Some breeders may have already proven certain sires and dams to be free of this hidden defect, but each new hypo from unknown heritage will have to be bred a few times to a known carrier in order to prove its genotype.

There is a third type of hypo (sometimes known as "Hypo C") that has been proven to be incompatible with the other known types. It was known originally as the trans (transparent) hypo but more recently has been referred to as a lava corn. The 2004 season presented an unprecedented

Hypomelanism has also shown up in Great Plains rat snakes.

cooperative test breeding trial between several different herpetoculturists hoping to unravel the genetics of several lines of hypo corns. Lavas were test bred to standard hypos, sunkissed (hypo Okeetees), ultra hypos, and "dreams" (another possibly new hypo-looking variant mentioned below). All hatchlings were normals, proving that lava is a distinct type incompatible with the others.

Lavas originated from some wild-caught corns from Jasper County, South Carolina, that were sold by Gordon Schuett to Joe Pierce of California in 1992. The hypos that resulted from those corns (much like the ultrahypo lines) have a somewhat different look from the other two types, a kind of milky translucence to the black pigments. They generally look lighter in color overall than other hypos,

Okeetees have spawned their own strain of hypomelanism, leading to a brilliant line coined "sunkissed"/ "sunkist" corns.

171

almost like dark amelanistic corns with dark eyes. This line has already been crossed into anerythristics, resulting in a combination known as ice ghost. Joe Pierce and other breeders are in the early stages of combining it with other simple recessive morphs such as charcoal, lavender, and caramel, and it appears that this hypo may produce very bright and different-looking multi-trait animals.

A fourth hypo has been named "ultra hypo" (or "Hypo D") and produces corns so lacking in melanin as to appear almost, but not quite, amelanistic, without the pink eyes. The very attractive ultra hypos have been proven to be incompatible with the standard hypo, as well as the sunkissed and lava. However, many of the ultras also carry the standard hypo gene in a heterozygous state, thus confusing the issue for novice breeders.

The lava corn may be the result of yet another kind of hypomelanism. This line is being investigated right now to determine its relationship to other known strains.

It is likely that there may be other incompatible hypos in the trade as well. Some breeders are marketing hypo-looking animals as "dreams," "pumpkins," "Christmas corns," "sunsets," and other names. To our knowledge, most have not been proven to be separate from the earlier hypos through extensive breeding trials. Rich Zuchowski feels he may have one or more new types but has not yet bred them to all of the known types.

To further confuse the issue, one of the four tested types of hypo genes may interact with amelanism in unusual ways and could even have a co-dominant (genes that interact with each other in neither a recessive nor dominant way) relationship with that trait. Names such as "ultramel" (an appearance intermediate between ultra hypo and amelanistic) may be heard more frequently as test breeding trials continue to unravel the secrets of hypomelanism.

Once breeders have sufficiently mixed up all of the hypo types, it will be very difficult for anyone to know which hypo they have until they have bred it with other known types. We have taken care to keep our own hypo Okeetees separate from the other known types to avoid this scenario for as long as possible, but unless totally closed colonies of all the hypo types are kept, double or triple hypos or hets will eventually sneak in and make things more difficult when trying to produce specific combinations.

Caramel

This morph is the creation of Rich Zuchowski, who noticed a locally caught female corn in a Cape Coral, Florida (on the lower southwestern coast), pet shop that exhibited enhanced yellow. The snake was essentially normal with a flush of straw yellow around reddish-brown blotches. He immediately recognized the potential of using it to start selectively breeding to develop a strain of special ultrayellow corns. He has taken these projects through several generations, some of which are addressed later. In effect he's accelerating the tendency away from orange toward hyperxanthism, more yellow than is normally seen in average *E. guttata.*

Rich's F1 offspring from crosses of the original snake to a snow, and later to an amelanistic, were all normal looking. This was reasonable evidence that the original yellowish female was heterozygous for neither type A anerythrism nor amelanism. When those F1 siblings were crossed, a handful of amelanistics resulted, some of which displayed somewhat enhanced yellow. Some of these hatchlings were initially assumed to be anerythristic and snow corns. The anerythristics tended toward brown instead of black, and the yellow pigment filled in slowly (as it usually does in young corns) to eventually show particularly intensely and

attractively in this morph. These are now known as caramel corns. The snows got much yellower, too, later being recognized as butter corns. There seems to be a new gene involved here that mimics or overshadows anerythrism in some ways, but it has also proven to be neither of the known forms of anerythrism, type A or charcoal. It is inherited as a simple recessive gene and under further intensive scrutiny as part of many ongoing breeding projects to uncover the true nature of its identity and the range of its uses in herpetoculture.

Recently, many breeders have noticed that offspring het for caramel or het for caramel and amel (butter) have had a certain yellowish look to them. This should not be possible if it is a simple recessive trait that only shows up in homozygous offspring. The point has been debated, and there is some consensus that the likely reason for the yellow showing up is that breeders have been keeping back the most yellow babies, regardless of the effect of the caramel gene itself. If this is true, future stock will be increasingly yellow because of conscious selective breeding. As breeding trials progress, a more definitive answer will reveal itself.

Lavender

Lavender is an oddly colored corn morph in which a pinkish purple-gray pattern is displayed against a paler grayish-white background, making it superficially look like a more attractive variation of anerythrism. In 1985, Rich Zuchowski hatched the first lavender corn as a single animal of an F2 clutch from a female that died egg-bound. The grandparents were a "snow" corn bred to a wild-caught normal corn from the Sarasota-Punta Gorda area of Florida's lower western coast. It looked like a normal baby corn at first, leading Zuchowski's wife, Connie, to call it mocha to describe its slightly unusual chocolate brown appearance as a hatchling. It proceeded to slowly change by losing the warmer reddish tones as it grew. This is almost the reverse of what happens in anerythristic corns when they get old and sometimes start turning a browner tone as reds and yellows slowly accumulate. The name lavender more accurately describes adults and has since emerged as the most universally accepted term after a lively debate raged via the Internet for over a year about its heritage.

As the gene was spread to other collectors hidden in some normal-looking by-products of other projects, its latent variability resurfaced in John Albrecht's and Dan Thomasco's breedings. They include backgrounds that often show an orangish to pinkish tone in the prettiest specimens, and the dorsal blotching sometimes takes on a purplish to grayish cast.

Some lavenders from the start of the project have had eerily attractive red eyes that almost glow with an inner

Lavender is the very appropriate name that describes this corn morph in which the entire snake takes on a light purplish cast, and sometimes glowing pink eyes too.

light. This point was missed at first and only later noticed by Jeff Yohe and brought to the attention of Rich Zuchowski about his snakes. Recent efforts have shown that this eye color seems to be inherited separately from lavender since it has shown up in ghost corns, too. The ruby-eye trait's pink cast is amplified when combined in the same animal with recessive hypomelanism. Similar traits have been found in mice and rats, and this may prove to be the first corn snake trait that targets only the eyes for its color effect.

Southwest Florida—Weird Gene Reservoir?

In poring over the case histories of all these morphs of corns, a curious connection has become apparent. The lavender strain behind the pink snow, white snow, and pearl corn was descended from an ancestor from coastal southwestern Florida. This is essentially the same region of origin of our original Pine Island female corn that introduced charcoal (type B anerythrism) that went on to make blizzards and our zigzags. Most of the early, more common type A anerythristic specimens also came from an inland region of southwestern Florida. The legacy compounds! The caramel line, whose original purveyor was also from that same geographical area, seems to carry a new gene affecting red and yellow pigment that's interacting strangely with other known *E. guttata* morphs.

Southwestern Florida seems to be a recurring link in all these cases. Can these facts somehow be parts of the same puzzle? Could a new mutant gene (or genes) exist that's actually widespread in populations of corns from a broad portion of lower coastal southwestern Florida—one that has crept into collections via several avenues to leave us presently confused? Is it also recessive, or just hidden by the other colors we're tossing into the stew before we know what we really have? Could it be something affecting those iridophores that we haven't mentioned since the opening comments on amelanistic corns, or is it something else entirely?

Not to purposely confuse the issue, the caramel corn history in particular is interesting in a related way since it's been proven that some caramel corns are in fact heterozygous for type A anerythrism, which was introduced back with the first breeding of the original yellowish caramel female to a male snow corn by Rich Zuchowski. This is analogous to the situation with his lavender corn line and is also, not coincidentally, the case with our own charcoal corn in which we too chose a male snow corn in the first mating to explore its heritage.

The early introduction of known recessive ingredients, such as type A anerythrism, has seemingly clouded our ability to decipher the exact recipes of some of the new morphs popping up a decade or more later. While it will continue to complicate our understanding of the genetic heritage of some emerging corn snake lines, there was a purpose to the original madness. The use of snow corns as initial mates was a sort of litmus test at the time to see if newfound snakes were exhibiting (in disguised form) or were carrying genes for the aberrant traits already familiar to us. Since there were not nearly as many different traits around in the mid-1980s as there are today, the two common ones, amelanism and type A anerythrism, were easiest to test for by simply crossing a snow corn to the newcomer. Then their F1 offspring were backcrossed a couple of years later to observe what turned up in the F2 generation.

Using totally normal-looking corns from distant origins as first mates, so as to avoid specimens possibly heterozygous for the traits we were investigating, would have also been nice to do as a backup strategy. We both might have exercised that option, too, except for the fact that all three original corns that got us working with the three morphs noted above were females. Had they been males, they could have been crossed out to multiple females, including normals and snows, allowing us to gauge the phenotypic and genotypic effects and relationships with other morphs sooner.

Despite which experimental path was chosen then, the fundamental point to be made here is the necessity to determine whether new corns suddenly showing up are really new genetically or just look different. This is particularly relevant today since many corn morphs haven't been around long enough yet to be seen in all their myriad forms. It reminds us of those fabled blind men feeling and describing different parts of the elephant, thinking they are "seeing" the whole picture. In the meantime, more and more herp hobbyists are jumping the gun and tagging new names on slightly divergent specimens of preexisting morphs. Some do it in the zeal to create something new and coin a name; others are dominated by the fervor to gain commercial marketing advantages. Without the benefit of having tested the "new" traits in breeding trials with known genetic variants, preferably over several generations, relationships are becoming increasingly hazy.

It's definitely too early to draw any firm conclusions about all the mysteries of *E. guttata* genetics until some very meticulous soul decides to devote some serious time to unraveling the dynamics of the interwoven genetic relationships. If we get nothing else out of this, it's irrefutable that the lower western coast of Florida has been the source of a number of extraordinary genes in *E. guttata*. Don't forget, that region also gave us hypomelanism and motley, too!

Piebaldism, Calico, and Related Traits

Piebaldism is a generic term for abnormal pigmentation that results in variously sized white areas replacing part of the usual color and pattern. In some individuals the white areas may dominate most of the body, leaving only tiny telltale spots and flecks of red, yellow, and black. Other specimens display unusually enlarged white borders to the dorsal blotches with additional scattered unpigmented splotches over their lengths.

Piebaldism was first noticed by us in a female specimen of *E. guttata* in the private collection of Dwain Collings of Tucson, Arizona, in the mid-1980s. She was reputedly collected in the Florida Keys. The white blotches did not cover more than about ten percent of her body as best as we recall. She produced some normal-looking F1 offspring,

Piebaldism is rare; when it occurs, it most often appears as small irregular patches of white amidst otherwise normal coloration. It exists as a small neck patch on this normal wild-caught corn (above) and as lateral splotches near the tail of a bloodred corn.

which were raised and bred together and back to the mother in a cooperative venture between us and Bern Bechtel, among others, during the 1980s. Reproductive trials resulted in only normal-looking progeny after two years of crossing the hopeful gene carriers among themselves. As the trait appeared not to be heritable, we gave up and dispersed the "hopeful hets" as just captive-bred normal corns. It seemed to be a potentially exciting trait that just wasn't meant to be. At least that's what we thought at that point.

Jillian Cowles in Arizona continued the project longer than anyone else, eventually demonstrating with some of her F2 generation that there's a built-in time delay of two to

"Calico" is a problematical anomaly that starts out 'hidden' as normal corn coloration. Snakes with this defect lost color over random areas of their bodies as they aged. Genetic deformities have so far accompanied this trait and hampered developing a problem-free bloodline. Efforts persist on the project.

The ruby freckled corn's establishment into herpetoculture has been hampered by the fact that its inheritance pattern remains a mystery. Under its influence, snow corns, the morph it appeared in first, have slowly gained indiscriminately spaced red splotches with age.

three years before the piebald effect starts to manifest itself. When it finally did show up, white splotches appeared, sometimes gradually, but other times immediately, when the skin was shed. It was always accompanied by a blistering distortion of the scales at those sites, which seemed to be a function of the pigment disruption process. This occurred in nonpiebald offspring of that bloodline, which left hope that it could be bred out of the strain to leave healthy corns with only the highly variable color anomaly intact. The delayed onset of the whitening until after maturation, combined with the fact that it occurred mostly in females, curiously paralleled the effects of a human condition called lupus, including its occasional fatal results.

Other corns have turned up with a white patch or two. We even own a locally caught one ourselves, but so far nobody has been able to predictably produce healthy piebald or calico corns. We are encouraged by the fact that a type of piebaldism already exists in ball pythons (*Python regius*), in which it's been reliably demonstrated to be passed on recessively. The challenge of this project embodies the spirit of modern herpetoculture.

Another new corn snake anomaly came to our attention quite recently. In 1996 Joe Hiduke and Bill Brant hatched two male snow corns that have small, scattered patches of pure red emerging randomly over their bodies. These ruby-

The paradox corn, unlike the ruby-freckled corn, hatched with the aberration shown. It also has faint hints of black on its head. Its genetics are still not clearly understood.

freckled corns resulted unexpectedly from the routine mating of two standard snow corns. As hatchlings they looked like typical snow corns—plain white and translucent—and only started developing a few red scales after a couple of skin sheds had occurred. The size of the red spots has slowly increased, sometimes in random clusters, leading Joe and Bill to retain the snakes so progress of the transformation could be monitored. Both males matured in 1998 and fathered offspring for the first time. They have been extremely hardy and healthy and have shown no evidence of any scalation defects in the red areas or elsewhere. The genetics and degrees of eventual red coverage in this morph are still in the infancy of study. Mention of them is included here purely because of their obvious, but reverse, resemblance to the cases of piebaldism discussed above.

Since those first breedings, many progeny have been produced, and the two male snows are now great-grandfathers. Unfortunately, the effect has not proven to be a simple recessive trait. In 2003, two ruby-freckled adults were bred together for the first time at Gourmet Rodent. Their offspring were all normal-colored snows, as have been all of the offspring from the supposed het babies of the original males. Strangely, other ruby-freckled babies have popped up in the collection and have not been directly related to the original males, as far as can be determined. The heritability of this trait is unknown at this time.

This juvenile came from two bloodreds crossed together. It seems to possess random swatches of hypomelanistic influence.

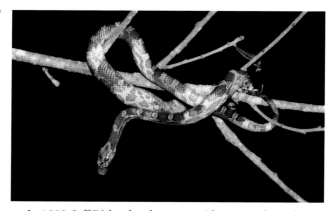

In 1993, Jeff Risher bred a snow with a striped purchased from two different sources and thus presumably unrelated. Keeping back one pair of typical amelanistics from that clutch, he produced (1996 to 2002) approximately 123 babies of the expected assortment of amels, stripes, snows, and others. Among them was one he named "paradox" because she was a snow with some black pigment on her head. In 2002, the paradox was bred to her father and two of the amels produced also showed some black pigment on their heads. It should be very interesting to see what the future holds for these black-tinged amels and snows.

A few other individual corns have turned up randomly in various breeding colonies sporting bits of white, black, red, or hypomelanistic touches where they should not have had those colors at all. Although the genetics are not yet known for these animals, their existence points toward a lot of fun and vexation for the future of corn snake breeding!

Pattern Mutations

Coloration is only one aspect of a corn snake's appearance. Completely separate sets of genes control how the markings will be shaped. These genes are subject to the same selective influences as color, making pattern the second major trait undergoing modification at the creative hands of both Mother Nature and herpetoculturists. The following types of pattern anomalies exist in E. guttata that we are aware of at present.

Motley/Striped

Motley is an inherited anomaly that tends to elongate and join the dorsal blotches together. They can range in appearance from a ladderlike pattern of fused or partially fused blotches to a complete and perfectly even stripe down the entire dorsal surface of the snake. The results can be extremely variable! It's not unusual for the pattern to form stretches of partial stripes that meld into normal or partially fused blotches at random areas across the back.

The distribution of the black pigment dorsally seems to be affected, too. Very rarely are the blotches outlined in black as in many normal corns, and these snakes often appear to possess less black in general. This often creates a hypomelanistic effect in normally colored motley corns.

The pattern disruption also affects the side blotches, basically erasing or absorbing them, or at least reducing them to scattered remnants of spots and streaks. Motley also exerts a secondary influence in which the black ventral checkerboarding pattern is completely or nearly completely lost. An interesting note is that the checkerboard was always completely absent in past generations, but recently some newer motley generations have been noted with up to 5 percent black on their bellies, and this seems to be on the increase. Some specimens have various shades of reds and oranges present on the belly; others are plain white with a light peppering.

The motley trait is barely noticeable in this corn whose blotches are both banded and elongated.

Motley corns typically have stretched dorsal saddles with the tendency to connect strongest closer to the head. This color variant is called the "pastel motley," the term "pastel" is usually applied to colorful yellowish-pink ghost corns.

The motley mutation cropped up spontaneously in many collections from stock tracing its origins to scattered localities along the lower western coast of Florida. Hillsborough, Pinellas, Manatee, and Sarasota counties, where *E. guttata* occurs in great abundance, produced the most examples from the wild that actually exhibited the trait too. But at least one motley specimen also came from around Adel, Georgia.

When isolated, small circles outlined in a darker hue are all that's left of the background between the connected blotches, we've heard this variation of motley marketed as a hurricane corn. The term chaos referring to angular or asymmetrically geometric patterns that have been spawned from motley/striped crosses bred out to normals; cubed has been coined for corns sporting particularly squared, isolated dorsal blotches of similar origins.

Jeff Risher has produced an attractive sunspot corn pattern from some breedings that included a striped corn ancestor, and those same experiments have also thrown patternless corns (discussed later). The sunspots look like what one might expect very low blotch count motleys to resemble, even though actual motleys were never used in the recipe.

Striped corn snakes have the appearance of a wide pale orange line down the centerline of the back, with narrow darker red ones flanking it. A second pair of darker lateral

stripes is often present, too, but they're usually less distinct and often broken into short dashes. The dorsal blotches are absent, although vestiges often occur on the tail and less frequently interspersed in the striped pattern on other parts of the body. Completely dorsally striped examples are rare, but they exist. The black ventral checkerboard pattern also disappears when this trait occurs.

Although corns with striped and motley patterns breed true in the sense that those traits do not beget normally patterned offspring when bred with each other, they don't always produce babies with exactly the same patterns as their parents, either. Striped and motley have proven to be pattern anomalies that are related to each other. Crossing the two together produces 100 percent oddly patterned offspring ranging in looks from long-blotched "barely motley" to more-or-less fully striped. The one constant was that all lacked the ventral checkerboard pattern. This suggests that striped and motley may both be alleles (versions of the same gene) and are co-dominant to each other when they exist together in the same animal. This means that either one alone is recessive when paired with a gene for normal corn snake pattern. But when the pair of pattern genes present in a corn is some combination of the motley and striped alleles, they'll be expressed as either motley, striped, or a mixture of the two. Rarely, if ever, will a fully striped baby be produced from mixing of the two. Even

in subsequent generations, the motley stripe has a different look from the pure stripes, usually evidenced by a changing width of the stripes instead of a constant width usually seen in the striped corns from Mike Nolan's strain. We and others have made crosses to test this many times since 1991, when Mike McEachern suggested the possibility. Thus, striped and motley corns appear to be different versions of the same trait genetically.

Motley, which we'll assume to include striped from here onward in the discussion, may hold the greatest potential for continued experimentation to produce new designer morphs of corn snakes in the future.

The bold sunspot pattern came from parentage that included striping, which may or may not be a link to motley genes as the factor behind the eye-catching design.

186

Banded

A banded pattern alteration in corns is currently being developed along several lines. It relies, at least in some cases, on the introduction of the motley gene. Don Soderberg has produced an impressive line of banded motleys that breeds true. When bred with typical unrelated motleys, his line produces all motleys of varying patterns. Other lines may rely on a distant *E. guttata emoryi* heritage or just many generations of selective breeding of pure *E. guttata*. The usual squarish or rectangular dorsal blotches expand sideways to form wrap-around, saddlelike markings that resemble elongated ovals draped across the snake's back. The goal is a corn snake with cleanly defined crossbands reaching from the ventral plates completely across the back in a series all the way down snake's length, much like some of the ringed milk snakes *(Lampropeltis triangulum)*. Saddleback is an alternative name also used for this look. Combining the banded pattern with the color attributes of his milk snake phase corns is one direction that Rich Zuchowski has sought to enhance the appealing effect that mimics true milk snakes of the northeastern United States Don Soderberg's crosses with Miami phase corns have taken the project down a related path toward a high contrast corn with bands boldly standing out from the ground color.

The enlarged blotches dominate on a banded motley corn.

Zigzag/Zipper

One source of the zigzag/zipper phenomenon was begun inadvertently in 1984 as a by-product from our project involving normally patterned corns, one being our original charcoal female from Pine Island, Florida. As we inbred for a few generations to investigate that new morph, we also noticed an increasing number of offspring with fused blotches. A few exhibited longer stretches of zigzaggy blotches that resembled a zipper. More accurately, it looks as if the usual square or rectangular mid-dorsal blotches had

Efforts are underway to breed "banded" corns with single big wrap-around saddles that absorb the side blotches and reach from belly to belly across the snakes' backs.

This normally colored corn is exhibiting a clean-cut zigzag pattern. The stripe seemingly wants to become a wide stripe made of connected blotches in some places along its back.

been split lengthwise and partially slid apart forward and backward, but remained attached at the corners. Pairing the most extreme examples soon got us offspring with up to 95 percent zigzagged patterns. They do not breed 100 percent true in the same sense that simple recessive traits breed true when bred together, but the more extreme specimens have generally produced a higher percentage of zigzags per litter and also individual specimens with larger percentages of the connected pattern on them than do less extreme specimens. Normally patterned hatchlings still appear from time to time in the line, too; they are especially prevalent when crossing normally patterned descendants of zigzags that would have been expected to be heterozygous for the trait. This suggests that the mode of inheritance is not simple and is far from being clearly understood to date. It appears to work more like a selectively bred trait. It is possible to breed two very ziggy adults together and get 100 percent normal-looking babies, although this usually happens when breeding adults from different bloodlines that look similar.

Rich Zuchowski has a somewhat divergent form in which the dorsal design is broken up into an unpredictable pattern of irregular blotching, streaks, and spots. He has coined the name aztec for it. It is an asymmetrical pattern of a different line of zigzags pioneered by John Albrecht as an offshoot of his work with the lavender corn project. We have since seen some of our zigzags diverge toward the

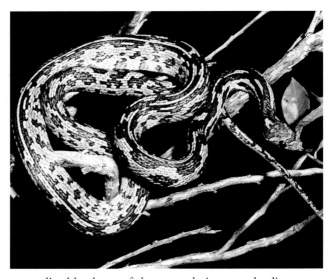

unpredictable chaos of the aztec design, too, leading us to suspect that the same gene(s) may be at work in both forms. Andy Barr is also working with another line of zigzaggy corns in which a very distinct, thick, wavy stripe undulates down the midline of the dorsum; it's not yet known if it represents a new inheritable pattern trait. It actually appears as a cleaner, more well-defined version that's bound to be popular in the future. It was created at least in part from our original zigzag strain crossed out to unrelated stock.

What may turn into a new pattern anomaly of the future is displayed by Don Soderberg's chocolate Emory's rat snake, discussed earlier under anerythrism. A high percentage of its dorsal blotches appear split apart diagonally, running down its entire length as a nearly parallel row of alternating smaller spots that are virtually the same size as the lateral blotches. That spotted effect has been inherited in the expected simple recessive mode along with the chocolate color aberration it first appeared with. It wouldn't be hard to imagine them as a zigzag pattern if they were just slightly connected, but maybe this new look will prove to be entirely different. Color variants heavily outnumber pattern variants in corns, so something new like this on the herpetocultural horizon is welcomed!

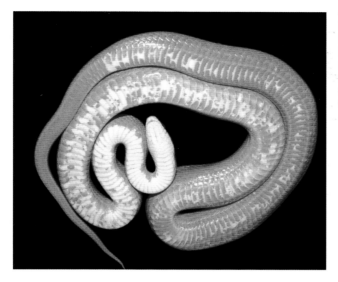

The ventrum of a bloodred corn lacks black checkerboarding; the amount of red suffusion may vary considerably.

Plain Belly

The absence of the ventral pattern of black geometric checkerboarding is less conspicuous than dorsal pattern abnormalities but has shown up independently in at least two morphs of corns. While the amount of ventral coverage by normal black markings can vary considerably between individuals in nature, the simple fact of whether it's present at all seems to be genetically controlled as an all-or-nothing trait. In early generations, this seemed to be a simple recessive in the case of bloodreds where the lack of belly blotching is clearly inherited independently of the eventual degree of unicolor dorsal redness in adults. However, it may be related to the diffused lateral pattern—more about that in the bloodred section. Intriguingly, we've had some offspring from bloodred × normal crosses that also lack virtually all of their ventral checkerboard pattern or have it reduced to mere hints concentrated along the edges of their ventrals, leaving the centers of their bellies essentially clear. In motleys/striped the patternless ventrum only occurs accompanying the dorsal anomaly, no matter to what degree it's expressed. We have never seen a plain belly in a heterozygous motley corn. Furthermore, offspring between

191

A new patternless / striped variant of rosy rat from the Florida Keys has given rise to "granite corns."

bloodreds and motleys have normally patterned ventrums indicating that the plain belly trait is non-allelic between the two anomalies.

Patternless

In addition to his paradox color anomalies, Jeff Risher also hatched twenty-four babies sporting various patternless versions of amels, anerys, and snows. The patternless specimens may also represent an extreme of the effect striping produces in certain virtually unicolored adults, but again it's not possible to state definitively yet.

Stephen Fowler and Craig Boyd own some very interesting specimens they call the granite morph. The finely speckled animals are derived from rosy rat snake (Florida Keys) stock that may be considered patternless by virtue of lacking definable blotched or saddled markings anywhere on their dorsums (backs). The same line has produced corns with a striped, patternless, or granite appearance, and examples of one or all of the morphs may be found in any given clutch. Their relationship to other striped and patternless morphs has not yet been demonstrated.

Mixing and Matching Morphs

The preceding color and pattern variants exist as singular traits, are generally reproduced following simple genetics, and already are involved in ongoing selective breeding efforts. Undoubtedly more new ones will surface to spice-up the number of variations possible in the near future. A few that we should expect are anomalies reducing yellow and red pigmentation on a par with hypomelanism. Possibly someone will find the opposite hyper versions (having abnormally excessive amounts of those pigments). The latter may already be here in bloodred (with red) and caramel corns (with yellow). New heritable traits like these are eagerly being sought to expand the number of paints on modern herpetoculturists' palettes.

Besides waiting for new aberrations to pop up and hoping that they're heritable, new corn morphs may be created artificially by combining two or more existing traits. Snow corns, presently the most familiar double recessive mutation, got the trend rolling initially not long after their second basic ingredient, type A anerythrism, appeared and made them possible. The desire to expand the mixing and matching is well underway today within thousands of collections worldwide. Fanciful names for the newly created phenotypes are being applied at a rate that makes it nearly impossible to stay current on them all and fully describe their genetics. Some are named without test breeding to similar existing morphs to determine whether or not they are different or if the new morph is even reproducible at all. Most of these new cultivars will be winnowed out as they fail to withstand the hatband test of popularity over time,

The snow corn was the first widely-bred double recessive trait. Its obvious extreme divergence from the colors of normal corns caught the public's fancy a quarter century ago when it first appeared.

Snow corns were named for their "frozen white" coloration, not their preference for winter basking. They lack black and red pigment.

but a few will manage to pass the test. Those will ultimately stick when a loyal following accepts them and strives to further intensify or otherwise change and improve the strain. Some that seem destined to last, or that just caught our eye, are illustrated in photos and are described below.

Snow

Snow corns were the first white snakes, and at the same time were the first double recessive snakes in history that were purposefully created in captivity. It was accomplished by the logical experimental step of combining the recessive genes for amelanism and anerythrism into one individual. When those traits occur simultaneously, neither black nor red pigments are present. That leaves only the iridophores and maybe some residual yellows to color the snake, creating an

The blotches appear with a more greenish tinge in certain individual snow corns, lending the name "green-blotched snow" to price lists occasionally.

essentially white specimen that still retains enough remaining subtle pigments to delineate the pattern easily. This came as somewhat of a surprise to the two creators, Glen Slemmer and Bern Bechtel, who weren't quite sure what to expect in the mid-1970s when both men strove to achieve the same results independently of one another; Slemmer won the race by a year.

Breeders have already started marketing the most extreme forms such as the green-blotched snow, in which the dorsal blotches exhibit a yellowish-green tinge that is

The prevalence of pinkish tones on and between the blotches has resulted in the trade name of "strawberry corn" for specimens such as this. Some might also call it a "bubblegum snow" though that name has historically been reserved for specimens with greenish-tinged blotches.

The opal (formerly called "pearl corn") is sometimes virtually pure white, but other times has vibrant pink or yellowish tones combined with white. It came about through combining lavender and amelanistic stock.

probably a result of interplay between light and the poorly understood reflective cell layer in most snakes' skins. A bubblegum snow is also being refined to emphasize the pink tones in the otherwise white background. They may be analogous to the strawberry snow being bred and marketed in England by Kevin Stevens. Hypomelanistic snow corns are homozygous for three different recessive traits and are being marketed as coral snows by Don Soderberg. Unfortunately, hatchling snow corns look almost identical. It may be a six-month or more wait after hatching to find out if snows selectively bred for such "gradually turned-on shades" will actually turn out as hoped.

Until a few years ago, all snow corns were derived from the common type A anerythrism. Inevitably, charcoals (type B anerythristics) were bred into the strain by Rich Zuchowski, John Cole, Art Meyer, and us just to see how it might differ, if at all. The charcoal corn's virtual lack of yellow had the rather dramatic effect of almost eliminating whatever delineated the blotches on snow corns, thus they appeared plain white. We dubbed this phase the blizzard corn—as in a blizzard, all you see is white. Alas, not all specimens grew up to be quite as pure white as we had hoped. Some examples still retained a trace of a yellow ring

Just as in a blizzard, all you see is white in the blizzard corn. Actually, minute traces of yellow sometimes creep into their patterns with age.

where the blotch would have been, whereas others possessed a faint shadow pattern only visible in strong light. It was almost as if a small dog had wandered through to soil the blizzard's purity! These tendencies toward yellowing aren't apparent in neonates because of the delay in yellow's formation in corns.

Don't forget the fact that even our original Pine Island female was apparently heterozygous for type A anerythrism, which may somehow be responsible for the lingering yellow of some blizzard corns or any other consequences of crosses in which it may have inadvertently participated.

Another strain of white corn was also investigated by John Albrecht and existed in at least two variations dubbed pink snow and white snow. Both are offshoots of Rich Zuchowski's lavender (mocha) corn line. The pink line looks like what might be expected from crossing amelanism and lavender, highlighting a rosy pink tinge. The other white line is a more or less pure white corn snake that may be a triple homozygous concoction combining lavender, amelanism, and type A anerythrism, and may be what used to be referred to as a pearl corn, a name that is seldom heard anymore. It shouldn't be confused with another recessive trait called leucism, which obliterates all color and pattern. The bright white strain of leucistic Texas rat snakes, *E. obsoleta lindheimeri*, is the best-known form of this rare trait today. Like true melanism, leucism has not occurred in *E.*

Butter corns are living proof that plenty of yellow is lurking under all the red and black of some strains of corns. They may also have a gene that actually enhances the amount and / or distribution of yellow pigment. No *E.g. emoryi* bloodlines were involved in its creation.

guttata yet to the best of our current knowledge. Still, some specimens of blizzard and amelanistic lavender corns become extremely white. Opal is the name most used for amel lavenders at this time.

Many different morphs of corns for this book, a cloud of uncertainty blew in about the various kinds of anerythrism and their roles in some of the multirecessive morphs. It's best to tackle the uncertainties after first digesting the discussions of the other corn morphs involving anerythrism that follow.

Butter

When caramel is combined with amelanism, the result is a corn that appears to be a hyperxanthic snow corn with golden yellow covering most of its body as an adult. Hatchlings start out rather white like baby snows with butterscotch blotches. That is to be expected since the intensity and bodily distribution of yellow pigment is never very apparent until any corn reaches at least a few months to a year in age. An adult butter corn resembles the most intensely yellow of creamsicle corns but is brighter and without the tendency to lean toward peachy oranges as creamsicles often do. Unlike creamsicles, these corns are not a subspecific cross involving the western race of corn snake, *E. guttata emoryi*. Rich Zuchowski has christened his creation with the trade name butter corn.

Amber corns are a combination of two recessive traits, caramel and hypomelanism.

Amber

The caramel high-yellow trait combined with hypomelanism produces amber corns, ranging from a golden amber to a pleasing light greenish-brown. By softening the masking influence of the black, the yellow wash is much more evident. This appears to be an ideal animal in which to acquire two interesting genes—caramel and hypomelanism—that have not yet been used to mix and match into all the other corn morphs. Recent ambers produced with the ultra hypo gene instead of the original hypo gene appear much closer to looking like butters but with darker eyes.

"Ultra amber" came from caramel crossed into the new form of "ultra hypo" instead of the older hypo line; initial results look promising.

They are a very attractive and unusual twist to the already popular old amber line.

Bloodred

The bloodred corn (also called a blood corn) is an interesting morph that falls somewhere between a wild corn and a designer morph of captivity. It was originally developed by Ed Leach in the 1970s and 80s, beginning with snakes he found in an area north of the city of Palatka in northeastern Florida. Many corns from there tend to be somewhat unicolor as adults—red blotches on a red-orange background, which attracted him to experiment with them further. Certain specimens had exceptionally pretty, brilliant red coloration with reduced (diffused) black borders around the blotches. In many, the lateral blotches are all but invisible. The tendency for the ground color to match the blotch color may be a form of hypererythrism (an abnormally excessive amount of red pigment), although it is inherited variably from individual to individual, not like a simple recessive trait.

When Ed inbred his early precursor bloodred stock, many offspring totally lacked the black ventral checkerboarding. They also displayed an intense and unicolor red dorsal coloration, extremely diminished black blotch outlines, and loss of the associated lateral blotching. The lack, or virtual lack, of ventral pattern seemed to be a simple recessive trait early in the breeding efforts, although

As adults, bloodreds of about five years of age or more appear ideally as solid red creatures with little or no trace of pattern, including having no black ventral spots or checks.

we have started seeing evidence of it in outcrossed corns more recently. The quality of the dorsal color and pattern and reduction of black outlining, on the other hand, occurred in every gradation of all the possibilities within the group, rather than as all-or-nothing traits. The two traits are not always completely linked—there are some outcrossed individuals that showed evidence of their bloodred heritage dorsally but did not inherit the lack of ventral pattern. However, it is generally accepted that both traits must be present for the animal to be designated as a traditional bloodred corn in the herp trade. It's also possible that more than two genes, not necessarily inherited as simple recessive genes, or multiple alleles of some genes, are involved in the inheritance of this complicated association of traits.

The amount of black "hidden" on a normal bloodred corn is best appreciated when much of it is removed, as in the hypomelanistic bloodred seen here side by side with a typical bloodred.

Recent debates have focused on calling bloodred a color mutation alone and whether the pattern mutation aspect (reduced black) should be recognized as separate. Part of what makes the bloodred anomaly so attractive is the intense red color, but just as important is the diffusion of the black pigment that makes up the pattern. A good example should exhibit a high degree of both factors, but it appears that the diffusion of pattern may be able to be inherited separately from the intensity of the red. We propose calling the reduction of pattern, especially the lateral pattern, as originally recognized in bloodred diffusion or diffused.

Breeders are working now to combine the bloodred pattern diffusion into the butter morph, hoping to work toward producing a unicolored golden yellow snake by removing the red color but retaining the faded pattern. Considering the enthusiasm and creativity of corn snake hobbyists, lavenders and others will surely follow.

Since its creation, the bloodreds have been outcrossed into amelanistic, anerythristic, hypomelanistic, and several other nonrelated bloodlines, as well as inbred to continue the pure strain. It should prove handy in intensifying the reds of other strains that haven't yet been explored much, analogous to the opportunities the caramel corn line offers with yellow. Sometimes this mixing produces heightened red in some offspring that could no longer be deemed pure

The crimson corn is a beefed-up Miami phase corn that's also hypomelanistic. Efforts to emphasize the boldness of the red blotches against the pale ground color are heightened by "wiping the slate clean of dirty wash" through the addition of the hypo gene.

bloodreds but turned out to be unusually beautiful in their own right. Outcrossing usually dilutes the purity of the solid red, so large numbers of offspring must be raised to see how it looks in nonjuveniles. Such larger scale efforts are necessary to be able to select the best generation of breeding stock for further reintensification of the original redness.

Crimson

Crimson is a new and improved cultivar of Miami phase corns by Rich Zuchowski. To brighten and clean up the red-orange blotches and the silvery ground color, hypomelanism was bred in to reduce the dirty wash of melanin over the entire body, while retaining enough for delineation of the blotches. Most crimsons do not retain a lot of the silvery background from the Miami phase, yet they look different from a typical hypomelanistic. The hypo Miami created by Don Soderberg emphasizes the silver-gray background color more than any of the crimsons we have observed.

Ghost

Combining hypomelanism and type A anerythrism produces a pale snake that exhibits a ghostly faded image of a normal corn, like a ghost. Many display delicate shades of lavender, pink, and yellow, enhanced and deepened by the

Ghost corns are as variable as any other strain of corn snake, evidenced by this exceptionally pale specimen at another end of the gamut.

contrasting grayish outlines in the pattern. The term pastel
has sometimes been applied to describe ghosts, especially
motley ghosts, with heightened pink and beige tones. The
subtler tones that some individuals develop will show only
after several months or more of age.

Although we first created the original ghost corns using
only type A anerythrism, we realize that others have
introduced charcoal to hypomelanism to come up with
similarly colored but distinctive-looking specimens. The
names charcoal ghost and phantom are being used to
distinguish the charcoal-based varieties. Their genetic
ancestry will become increasingly hard to track as many
people, including us, are already having difficulty
distinguishing them by looks alone. Once the various new
types of hypomelanism are used in ghosts, it should present
us with more choices of appearances, as well as more
frustration in trying to decide just which ghost will produce
more ghosts when mated with a particular individual.

Pewter

The combination of charcoal and the diffused pattern of
bloodreds yields pewter, a medium gray snake with dorsal
blotches that fade into the nearly identical ground color in

This large male pewter corn took on a more unicolored grey coloration the older it became, just as bloodreds get redder with age.

adults. The dorsal blotches lose their well-defined edges with age until large adults exhibit a cryptically blurred pattern that's almost hidden against the ground color. Some specimens exhibit a fine "dusting" of black, inviting the alternate name pepper corn for this double recessive trait. Considering its bloodred heritage, some adults display a more well-defined residual blotch pattern than others.

We're still not sure exactly how to classify the frosted look in corns. It adds a distinctive whitish speckling effect to the whole snake by concentrating the pigment of each scale on the central keel, especially within each blotch.

Frosted

We've tucked the frosted trait here for sheer lack of certainty about how to categorize it properly. The effect we've seen in several specimens of different colorations is for a pale speckling or highlighting to whiten the scales, particularly inside the dorsal blotches. The resulting frosty look adds a contrasting wash that's distinctive. One strain has its origins in the Tampa, Florida, region nearly two decades ago when some crosses were made between corns from Mike Falcon, Andy Barr, and John Cole. It involved an odd, locally-caught snake that was at first suspected of being a hybrid cross between a corn and a yellow rat snake, *E. obsoleta quadrivittata*. It was crossed to a snow corn that apparently also carried hypomelanism in the first generation of experimental breeding. It now appears that the mystery snake was not a hybrid, but instead an early hypomelanistic corn unrecognized at the time. The frosted look may be a product of its interaction with other recessive color reductions, but it's not yet fully clear how this trait intermingles and is inherited.

Combined Pattern Traits

Corns sometimes display two or more colors and combined pattern traits. The following images represent some of the most unusual and spectacular specimens.

Intergradation and Hybridization

The nominate race of corn snakes—*E. guttata guttata*—intergrades with the western races (*emoryi, meahllmorum, slowinskii*) west of the Mississippi River. Intergrades occur naturally where different subspecies of the same species meet geographically, and those animals breed together to throw offspring resembling the parents and everything in between them in looks. There are no serious biological barriers to prevent this from happening. Crossing individuals of the species *E. guttata* from New Jersey, Florida, Utah, and Mexico in captivity is still making intergrades, even if they would have never come in contact in the wild under normal circumstances. We think of this

Creamsicle motley corn.

phenomenon, tagged forced intergradation, as a by-product of our modern-day ability to bring far-ranging races of corn snakes together for experimental herpetocultural crosses.

Hybrids result from the mating of different species, technically an impossibility if the strict definition of species—a group of organisms that interbreed but are reproductively isolated from all other similar groups—is adhered to and believed to be infallible. Crosses between *E. guttata* and yellow rat snakes (*E. obsoleta quadrivittata*) have

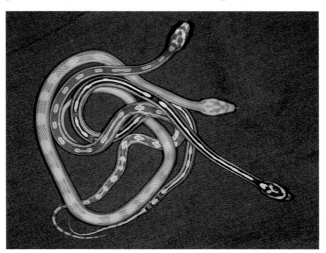

Three baby motley corns—anery, creamsicle, and amelanistic.

occurred in the wild and in captivity. Additionally, black rats (*E. obsoleta bairdi*, or just *E. bairdi*) have produced viable offspring with corns in collections. Corns have also been tricked into copulating with other colubrid snake species and genera as well. One method involves switching prospective mates at the frenzied height of sexual excitement just prior to a normal intraspecies breeding.

Hypo Okeetee corn with strong yellow blotches.

Several hatchling bloodreds in 2003, both normal and hypo examples, sported unusually pale heads. We'll use them to selectively breed for enhancing that trait in future generations to see what extreme it might achieve.

Hi-white amelanistic corn.

Banded candycane corn.

Striped ghost corn.

The jury is still out on the genetics of this "confetti corn."

Hypo lavender corn.

Amelanistic corn with traces of black pigment—very odd.

"Freckled ghost" corn bearing spotty red pigment patches—also very odd.

Patternless anery corn.

Anery hurricane motley.

Striped sunglow corn.

Motley sunglow corn.

Albino chocolate Great Plains rat.

Motley / striped Miami phase corn.

Baby striped bloodred corn.

"Jungle corn" is the name bestowed upon hybrid crosses between corn snakes and California king snakes. That species cross seems to be the first one accomplished in the late 1980s.

AFTERWORD

Corn Soup: Challenges Beyond the Basics for Tomorrow's Herpetoculturists

With researching the 2004 update of our book, it was even more apparent than before that unraveling (and even keeping track of) the complexities of a burgeoning number of worldwide breeding efforts with *E. guttata* has become a daunting task. This is primarily due to the vast numbers of newcomers and players in the hobby. Finding the genetics inscrutable, most of them make little or no attempt at formally documenting the "recipes" of the crosses they're doing. We'd like to say there's no harm in that, but such is not entirely the case.

The huge and growing influx of new hobbyist breeders is attracted to corn snakes to have fun with them. Those who truly wish to carefully experiment and innovate on a more serious level are, more often than not nowadays, realizing that they must heavily rely on starting their projects with "corn soup." Most pet corn snakes available today are derived from captive breeding projects going back, at the very least, several generations. That fact virtually assures that they come with mixed genealogies one can barely guess at. Inevitably, projects will encroach upon each other. Similar-looking phenotypes will merge until it's impossible to disentangle individual traits from one another anymore. Unless starting from scratch with wild-caught stock, the odds are stacked heavily against anyone getting breeders with fully known genetic backgrounds upon which to base future crossings. The following analogy may better illustrate the growing conundrum.

Suppose, while rummaging through your recently departed grandmother's kitchen, you suddenly notice an aroma you remember from those nostalgically wonderful meals you had at her house as a kid. Then you discover a nearly empty jar of the secret seasoning blend she always used to make her cooking so delicious. You recall she made it from scratch from an old family recipe passed down through the generations. Too bad she kept the recipe stored only in her memory.

You're anxious to make more of that gastronomic additive you crave, but you have only the clues of the several dozen bottles of herbs and spices on her shelves. Since Granny grew most of her own seasonings in her garden and knew them intimately, she never felt it necessary to label those containers' contents. You can't tell what each one is, so you're forced to start recombining unknown powders and flakes at random ratios, adding and deleting some at each trial. You don't even know if she used all those ingredients or just some of them. Working blindly, how long would it take to exactly recreate her magical concoction?

One way to attack the dilemma would be to finely sort the last of her original mix and try to identify the granules under a microscope. A better way might be to have samples of each chemically analyzed or DNA-tested in a lab. Both methods require special equipment and expensive techniques. It's simply beyond most people's wills and means.

Maybe technology will soon provide us with a reasonably priced way to discover the genotype of our corn snakes via DNA testing, but don't count on it happening before the methodology has been perfected for numerous more urgent things such as treating humans' multifarious health needs. Until then, we and a handful of vigilant breeders will conscientiously keep careful records that we hope will preserve some assurance of predictability in future breeding projects. The deteriorating situation really begs someone to initiate a pedigree system based on an isolated collection to maintain all the pure recessive traits intact.

The forecast is for increasing cloudiness tracking the genetic histories of corn snakes. More and more chefs will inadvertently contribute to the mélange. Corn snake populations will continue to pyramid at the discretion of pet keepers who are not actually herpers and see no need to concern themselves with anything deeper than making a lot of cool corns that sell or swap easily.

Some have expressed the concern that the end concoction might resemble the same outcome as when we whimsically scribbled all our crayons into one thick, gummy brown smudge—resulting in a nondescript (and not very attractive) corn snake with the appeal of burnt toast. That worry, at least, is unrealistic because mankind's eternal appreciation of and quest for beauty will always prevail. It automatically turns away from spawning more nondescript morphs than can be temporarily absorbed by stamp collectors seeking the new fashion of the year, something different even if it's unattractive. The hatband test will assure that future E. guttata, in all its amalgamations to come, remains a species renowned for its beauty.

APPENDIX

Association of Reptile & Amphibian Veterinarians (ARAV)

This international nonprofit organization of more than 1,300 professionals and interested individuals is devoted to improving herp veterinary care, husbandry, and breeding through education, exchange of ideas, and research. They publish an informative bulletin, hold annual conferences, and maintain a directory on the Web site that helps people locate herp-savvy vets near their homes across the United States and around the world. Membership in ARAV is open to anyone.

Contact: ARAV, c/o Wilbur Amand, VMD, P.O. Box 605 Chester Heights, PA, 19017. (610) 358-9530. http://www.arav.org.

Herp Vet Connection

The Herp Vet Connection's Web site is maintained by herp keepers who have joined together to compile a list of veterinarians with herp experience. http://www.herpvetconnection.com

Pet Industry Joint Advisory Council (PIJAC)

PIJAC is the world's largest pet trade association that supports or opposes enactment of legislation and regulations in the best interest of the animals, the pet-owning public, and the pet industry. Its sworn mission is to ensure the availability of companion animals, including herps, to sustain the entire pet industry. It also focuses on education, information, and governmental issues involving pet stores, companion animal supply and restrictions, and obstacles to pet ownership. PIJAC fights for all against those who want to stop reptile keeping. Join at http://www.pijac.org.

Corn Snake Progeny Predictor

Noel "Mick" Spencer has created and made available a computer program that allows you to plug in data about your E. guttata parent stock to predict the expected ratios and patterns of their offspring. This will undoubtedly save many people a lot of time and befuddlement in finding fast answers to questions such as, "What do I get if I cross…" The handy Windows program can be downloaded at http://home.comcast.net/~spencer62/cornprog.html.

Serpwidgets' Genetics Info & Tutorial

Charles Pritzel's extensive Web site makes it easy to understand corn snake genetics in depth. The site uses clearly explained language and step-by-step Punnett square examples using familiar snake color and pattern traits. http://serpwidgets.com/Genetics/genetics.html.

REFERENCES

Applegate, R. 1992. *The General Care and Maintenance of Milk Snakes*. Lakeside, Calif.: Advanced Vivarium Systems.

Barnard, S. M., T. G. Hollinger, and T. A. Romaine. 1979. "Growth and Food Consumption in the Corn Snake, *Elaphe guttata guttata* (Serpentes: Colubridae)." *Copeia*, no. 4: 739-741.

Bechtel, H. B. 1978. "Heredity of Pattern Mutation in the Corn Snake, *Elaphe guttata*, Demonstrated in Captive Breedings." *Copeia*, no. 4: 719-721.

———. 1989. Color Mutations in the Corn Snake, *Elaphe guttata guttata*: Review and Additional Breeding Data. *Journal of Heredity* 80 (4): 273–276.

———1995. Reptile and Amphibian Variants–Colors, Pattern, and Scales. Malabar, Fla.: Kreiger Publishing.

Greenwald, O. E., and M. E. Kanter. 1979. "The Effects of Temperature and Behavioral Thermoregulation on Digestive Efficiency Rate in Corn Snakes (*Elaphe guttata guttata*)." *Physiological Zoology* 52 (3): 398–408.

Greenwald, O. E., and M. E. Kanter. 1979. "The Effects of Temperature and Behavioral Thermoregulation on Digestive Efficiency Rate in Corn Snakes (*Elaphe guttata guttata*)." *Physiological Zoology* 52 (3): 398–408.

Kauffeld, C. 1957. *Snakes and Snake Hunting*. Garden City, N.Y.: Hanover House.

———.1969. Snakes: *The Keeper and the Kept*. Garden City, N.Y.: Hanover House.

Klingenberg, R. 1993. *Understanding Reptile Parasites*. Lakeside, Calif.: Advanced Vivarium Systems.

Mader, D. R., ed. 1996. Reptile Medicine and Surgery. Philadelphia, Pa.: W.B. Saunders.

Mattison, C. 1998. Keeping and Breeding Snakes. 2nd ed. London: Blanford Press.

McEachern, M. J. 1991. *A Color Guide to Corn Snakes Captive-Bred in the United States.* Lakeside, Calif.: Advanced Vivarium Systems.

————.1991. *Keeping and Breeding Corn Snakes.* Lakeside, Calif.: Advanced Vivarium Systems.

Muir, J. H. 1981. Two Unusually Large Egg Clutches From a Corn Snake, *Elaphe guttata guttata. Bulletin of the Chicago Herpetological Society* 16 (2): 42–43.

Pritzel, C. 2004. "The Buyer's Guide to Cornsnake Morphs." Privately published. http://cornguide.com.

Rossi, J., and R. Rossi. 1996. *What's Wrong With My Snake?* Lakeside, Calif.: Advanced Vivarium Systems.

Schulz, K. D. 1996. *A Monograph of the Colubrid Snakes of the Genus Elaphe Fitzinger.* Czech Republic: Koeltz Scientific Books.

Slavens, F. L., and K. Slavens. 1998. *Reptiles and Amphibians in Captivity—Breeding, Longevity, and Inventory.* Seattle, Wash.: Slaveware.

Smith, G. C., and D. Watson. 1972. "Selection Patterns of Corn Snakes, *Elaphe guttata*, of Different Phenotypes of the House Mouse, *Mus musculus." Copeia* no. 3: 529-532.

Witwer, M. T., and A. M. Bauer. 1995. Early Breeding in a Captive Corn Snake (*Elaphe guttata guttata*). *Herpetological Review* 26 (3): 141.

INDEX

A

adults, 15, 56–58
Albrecht, John, 189
alertness/attentiveness, 19–20
ants, 125–126
Applegate, Bob, 111

B

bacterial overgrowth
    (intestinal), 127–128
Barr, Andy, 206
basking, 50
Bechtel, Bern, 195
behaviors: basking, 50;
    defensive, 22, 34; of escaped
    snakes, 38–39; feeding,
    59–60, 67; mating, 92–93;
    tail vibration, 33
bicephalism (two heads), 114
bites (of snakes), 33
bites (rodent to snake), 60,
    133–134
Black, Adam, 119
blisters/discoloration, 134–135
body defects/scars, 20–21
Boyd, Craig, 192
Brant, Bill, 119, 180–181
breeders, 24–25. See also
    color/pattern variations
breeding: determining breeding
    time, 89–94; double-
    clutching, 117–119; egg-
    binding, 136–140; future of,
    215–217; genetics, 152–155;

gestation/egg-laying,
    95–100; hatching, 109–110,
    113–114; housing neonates,
    114–116; incubating eggs,
    102–113; infertility, 95;
    insect pests, 111–113;
    longevity, 16–17; pre-
    breeding conditioning,
    83–89; premature hatching,
    140; reabsorption of eggs,
    116–117; recording
    reproductive data, 119–120;
    sexing, 78–83
brumation (hibernation),
    85–87

C

caging. See housing
candling (for egg fertility), 102
candling (sexing method), 81
captive-bred versus wild caught,
    22, 23–24
captivity, stresses of, 140–143
chain feeding, 69
characteristics of cornsnakes,
    8–9, 11, 15
choosing a snake: age, 22;
    history of snake, 21–22;
    signs of health/illhealth,
    19–21; sources for
    acquiring, 23–27;
    temperament, 21–22;
    transportation/shipping,
    25–27
clutch sizes, 99–100
Cole, John, 206
Collings, Dwain, 178
color/pattern variations: amber,
    199–200; amelanism,
    156–162; anerythrism,

162–166; banded pattern, 187; bloodred, 200–203; butter, 198; caramel, 173–175; combined pattern traits, 206–213; crimson, 203; frosted, 206; future of breeding, 215–217; genetics, 152–155; ghost, 203–204; hatband test, 151, 217; hypomelanism, 166–173; intergradation and hybridization, 206–213; lavender, 174–176; mixing and matching morphs, 192–206; motley/striped pattern, 183–186; naturally occurring morphs, 146–151; patternless, 192–193; pewter, 204–205; piebald/calico/related traits, 178–182; plain belly pattern, 191–192; range in, 144–146; snow, 194–198; southwestern Florida link, 176–177; zigzag/zipper pattern, 188–190

commercial diets, 60–63
Coote, Jon, 63
Cowles, Jillian, 179
Crytosporidium, 29

D
Damm, Norm, 157
dealers, 24–25
dehydration, 47, 109. *See also* humidity
digestive disorders, 126–131
diseases/disorders: blisters/discoloration, 134–135; Crytosporidium, 29; digestive disorders, 126–131; egg-binding, 136–140; finding a veterinarian, 121; mouth rot (stomatitis), 135–136; parasites, 21, 29, 122–126, 129–131; premature hatching, 140; ragged sheds, 46; respiratory infections, 21, 136; retained eye caps, 46–47; salmonellosis, 131–132; skin ailments, 132–135; snout injuries, 36; stress, 140–143
domestication, 17–18, 32–34

E
egg-binding, 15–16, 136–140
egg-laying, 95–100
Elaphe genus, 10
enclosures. *See* housing
Enge, Kevin, 161
escapes, 35, 38
euthanasia, 76–77
eye caps, 46–47

F
Falcon, Mike, 206
fecal exams, 29
feces/defecation, 20, 55
feeding: after egg-laying, 98–99; behavior, 59–60; during breeding season, 90–91; coaxing stubborn hatchlings, 69–76; digestive problems, 126–131; frozen prey/commercial diets, 60–63; gravid females, 95; increasing meal size, 68–69; live versus pre-killed, 65;

multiple snakes in an enclosure, 40; neonates, 116; of new snakes, 28; prey items, 55–56; schedule (adults and hatchlings), 56–58; size of prey, 55; Snake Steak Sausages, 62; stimulating with scent, 65–68; vitamin/mineral supplements, 64–65; when to offer, 64–65

females, 15–16, 78–83. *See also* breeding

fertile eggs, 100–102

finding an escaped snake, 38–39

force-feeding, 73–76

Fowler, Stephen, 192

G

genetics, 152–155. *See also* color/pattern variations

growth/size, 14–16

H

handling, 22, 29, 33–34

hatching eggs, 106, 140

hatchlings: defense behaviors, 22; disadvantages of buying, 23; feeding, 56–58, 69–76; housing, 36

Hazel, Mark, 16–17

health, signs of, 19–21

Hemens, Adrian, 114

hemipenes, 78–79, 80–82

hibernation (brumation), 85–87

Hiduke, Joe, 119, 138, 180–181

hot rocks, 51

housing: building a cage, 36; heating, 50–52; help for

shedding, 44–47; live plants, 49–50; neonates, 114–116; of new snakes, 28; number of snakes per enclosure, 39–41; shelters/hide boxes, 42–44; size of enclosure, 35–36; substrates, 41–42; water and humidity, 47–49

Humane Society of the United States (HSUS), 31

humidity, 44–45, 91–92, 104–105, 111

Hurley, Connie, 127

husbandry, 48, 117–118

I

ill health, signs of, 19–21. *See also* diseases/disorders

inbreeding, 154–155

incubating eggs, 102–113

infertile eggs, 100–102

infertility, 95

insect pests, 111–113

intelligence, 17–18, 34

isolation/quarantine, 29–30, 121–122

J

Jacobson's organ, 59–60

juveniles, prey items, 55

K

Kauffeld, Carl, 147–148

Krick, Mike and Linda, 158

L

Laszlo, Joseph, 53

Leach, Ed, 200–201

legal issues: buying/keeping snakes, 30–32; Georgia state

laws, 30–31; Lacey Act (shipping/transport), 27
length, 15–16
lighting, 52–54, 142–143
longevity, 16–17

M

MacInnes, Rob, 105
males, 16, 78–83. *See also* breeding
McEachern, Mike, 186
Miami phase morphs, 149–150
milk snake phase morphs, 150
mineral supplements, 63–64
mites, 21, 122–124
morphs. *See* color/pattern variations
mouth rot (stomatitis), 135–136
muscle tone, 20
mutations. *See* color/pattern variations

N

Nolan, Mike, 186

O

Okeetee corns, 147–149
ovulation, 89–90

P

Pantherophis genus, 11
parasites, 21, 29, 122–125, 129–131
pattern mutations, 182–192
patterns. *See* color/pattern variations
Pellicer, Mark, 100
People for the Ethical Treatment of Animals, 31

Pierce, Joe, 171
Pinkie Pump, 76
plants, live, 49
popping (sexing method), 80–81
pre-breeding conditioning, 83–89
premature hatching, 140
probing (sexing method), 81–82

Q

quarantines for new snakes, 28–30

R

recording reproductive data, 119–120
regurgitation, 57–58, 126
reproduction, size and, 14–16
respiratory infections, 21, 136
retained eye caps, 46–47
Risher, Jeff, 182, 186, 192
rodents, sources for, 60–61

S

salmonellosis, 131–132
scars, 20–21
Scheidt, Vince, 157
Schuett, Gordon, 171
scientific names, changes in, 10–11
selling neonates, 116
sexing, 78–83
shedding, 20–21, 44–47, 95–96, 124, 135
shipping/transportation, 25–27
size/growth of snakes, 14–16
size of enclosures, 35–36
size of prey, 55–58

skin, 20–21, 132–135

Slemmer, Glen, 159, 161, 195

Snake Steak Sausages, 62

snout injuries, 36

soaking, 47–48

Soderberg, Don, 159, 169, 187, 190, 196, 203

species/subspecies, 10–14

stargazing, 170

Stevens, Kevin, 196

stools, 20

stress, 140–143

substrates, 41–42, 96–97, 103–104, 115

symptoms. *See* diseases/disorders

T

tails, 79

taming, 17–18, 32–34

taxonomy, 9–14

tease-feeding, 72–73

temperament, 17–18, 22–23

temperatures: for digestion, 57–59, 126; hatching, 109–110; heating methods, 49–52; incubation, 107; pre-breeding cooling, 83–89; providing a range (thermal gradient), 43–44

ticks, 21, 124–125

traits, genetic, 152–155

transportation/shipping, 25–27

treatment of illnesses. *See* diseases/disorders

Trumbower, Craig, 114

twins, 114

U

under-tank heaters, 50–52

V

Van Horn, George, 168

ventilation, 36–37

vitamin supplements, 63–64

W

Web sites: finding a veterinarian, 121; genetics information, 152; U.S. Fish and Wildlife Service, 27

weight, 20

wild-caught versus captive bred, 22–24

Y

Yohe, Jeff, 176

Z

Zuchowski, Connie, 175

Zuchowski, Rich, 150, 162, 169, 170, 173–174, 175, 176, 189, 190, 195, 199, 203

ABOUT THE AUTHORS

Kathy & Bill Love have kept and bred corn snakes since the early 1970s in southwestern Florida. Kathy still maintains a moderately large private collection of corn snakes at her home. She has numerous selective breeding projects running, but also actively sells her captive-bred progeny through her business CornUtopia, accessible via http://www.cornutopia.com.

Kathy is always interested in hearing about breakthroughs in corn snake herpetoculture, both in husbandry ideas and new color or pattern morphs for future updates to this book. You may contact her directly at kathy@cornutopia.com.

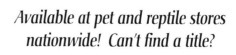